M·Shaw.

C000157865

BUTTERFLIES

Reader's Digest · National Trust

Nature Notebooks

BUTTERFLIES

Published by The Reader's Digest Association Limited, London,
in association with The National Trust

BUTTERFLIES
is a Reader's Digest Publication based upon
The Reader's Digest *Nature Lover's Library*
Copyright © 1984 The Reader's Digest
Association Limited, London

First Edition
Copyright © 1987
The Reader's Digest Association Limited
25 Berkeley Square, London WIX 6AB

ISBN 0-276-40947-7

All rights reserved.
No part of this book may be reproduced,
stored in a retrieval system, or transmitted in
any form or by any means, electronic,
electrostatic, magnetic tape, mechanical,
photocopying, recording or otherwise,
without permission in writing from the
publishers. This publication is not included
under licences issued by the Copyright
Licensing Agency

® READER'S DIGEST
is a registered trademark of
The Reader's Digest Association, Inc.
of Pleasantville, New York, USA

Typesetting by Vantage Photosetting Co.
Ltd, Eastleigh

Separations by Kera Graphics Ltd, London
and Mullis Morgan Ltd, London

Printed in Hong Kong

The cover illustration of red admirals at
Packwood House, Warwickshire, was
painted by Peter Barrett

Contents

The National Trust and its work

The National Trust, a private charity founded in 1895, could be said to be the oldest conservation organisation in the country. As well as caring for historic houses, castles and gardens, it owns 500,000 acres of land throughout England, Wales and Northern Ireland. It acquired its first nature reserve, Wicken Fen, as early as 1899 and by 1910 had 13 properties of particular wildlife value. It now owns some 50 Nature Reserves, over 400 Sites of Special Scientific Interest (SSSIs) and many other properties of great interest, not only for butterflies, but for a range of animal and plant communities.

The National Trust for Scotland, a separate organisation but with similar aims and objectives, was established in 1931. It owns 100,000 acres, including some of the finest mountain and coastal scenery in Scotland.

An Taisce – the National Trust for Ireland – was founded in 1946 and is the leading independent environmental body in the Republic of Ireland. Like the National Trust and the National Trust for Scotland, it concerns itself with the care and conservation of the countryside. It also maintains a number of properties for research purposes and for the enjoyment of visitors.

With one exception, all our resident butterfly species have colonies on National Trust land. These constitute a high percentage of the British populations of such rarities as Adonis blue, Glanville fritillary, Duke of Burgundy, silver-spotted skipper, small blue and small mountain ringlet. There are also important colonies of heath fritillary, high brown fritillary, marsh fritillary, purple emperor, Scotch argus and swallowtail. The one species not yet represented is black hairstreak.

More than 100 properties support colonies of our rarer species. Unfortun-ately, it is not possible for most of these sites to be included in this book, since the decline of many of our butterflies this century has been so dramatic that these remaining localities need protection from any unnecessary disturbance. Four species have become extinct since the middle of the last century – large copper, mazarine blue, black-veined white and, most recen-tly, the large blue (although this has now been re-introduced). A fifth, chequered skipper, is now extinct in England, and several species are at dangerously low levels, and are protected by law. Collect-ing pressure as well as habitat loss, are contributory causes to these losses and this is why we must avoid publicising where some species may be found. The National Trust bye-laws specifically prohibit the unauthorised capture of butterflies on National Trust land.

Butterfly conservation is not, however, an easy thing to achieve. Many important butterfly habitats are not self-maintaining and require active conservation work on the part of the Trust. Adonis blue, the chalk downland speciality, needs not only areas of short turf with good populations of its larval food plant and the presence of certain ants in order to breed successfully, but also tall patches of grass as sheltered roosting places. Other downland butter-flies, such as small blue and Duke of Burgundy similarly have very precise habitat requirements. Some of these requirements can appear contradictory but in practice the balance can be achieved by careful management of sheep grazing intensity, the strategic positioning of fence lines, allowing coarser grasses and scrub to remain in certain areas, and so on.

Many of our woodland butterflies were previously most numerous in woodlands managed as coppice-with-standards, the flowery clearings produced by this man-agement being particularly favourable. Serious declines of species such as the fritillaries have followed the decline of this form of woodland management. The Trust has re-established coppicing in many of its woods, not only to conserve these butterflies but also to help to con-serve a wide variety of other animals and plants associated with this type of woodland. Butterflies are very much sun-loving creatures and woodland species are no exception. Sunny clearings and rides with lots of nectar-producing flowers, are a great attraction, and these are an ideal situation for the butterfly spotter. The management of clearings and rides can be crucial in determining the numbers of butterflies which the wood will contain.

Other habitats requiring active man-agement include reedbeds for swallowtail and heathlands for silver-studded blue and grayling. Reed-cutting encourages the growth of milk parsley, the food plant for the larva of the spectacular swallowtail. This species also demonstrates the impor-tance of encouraging particular nectar-plants in the habitat, since the adult favours ragged-robin for feeding. Silver-studded blue and grayling both favour heathlands, with patches of bare ground where they can sun themselves. These patches were formerly created by grazing cattle but few heaths are still grazed. Nowadays the correct conditions can be maintained by cutting, burning and even by the tread of visitors' feet.

In addition to prohibiting the collect-ing of butterflies, the Trust's bye-laws also prohibit the unauthorised release of but-terflies, unless there is a sound basis for doing so. Only where a species has been lost from a particular site will the Trust consider permitting new stocks to be brought in, and then only when the site has been returned to a suitable condition

How to use this book

to support them. In this, the Trust follows the advice of the Joint Committee for the Conservation of British Insects in all such re-establishment projects.

Wherever possible, the populations of our rarer species are monitored – by our wardens or local naturalists. In this way we hope to have early warning of any declines, and hopefully sufficient time to identify the cause and correct it. Members can be of great assistance to the Trust in its conservation work by helping with this monitoring.

As already explained, sites for our rarer species are not included in this book. However, the sites which are listed have been selected to enable the visitor to see a wide range of our commoner species, at the right time of year, or where especially good numbers of a particular species can be seen. Visits to many of the sites listed in this book should enable the observer to appreciate not only the great responsibility which the National Trust has for the conservation of British butterflies but also the careful management work that is required to maintain their habitats.

Keith Alexander
Conservation Adviser's Office,
The National Trust

The British Isles are host to a wonderful variety of butterflies and many of these beautiful insects may be seen on the properties owned by the National Trust in Britain and Northern Ireland, The National Trust for Scotland and An Taisce in The Republic of Ireland. This book is a field guide to those butterflies, and it also includes a gazetteer of sites where you are most likely to see a particular species.

In the field guide section, Sites Guide boxes contain a brief general note on each species, together with an indication of where the butterflies may be seen. In some instances this note is followed by a sequence of numbers, and these act as the key to the book's dual function as an identification guide and sites gazetteer. The numbers (on pages 96–119) direct you to the sites where you may see the species.

The 'notebook' panels

At the foot of each species entry you will find a blank panel for making your own notes and sketches. Making notes of field observations enables you to identify the features of the species most easily, as well as making a record of your field trips. With butterflies it is often interesting if you try to identify what plants a butterfly feeds and rests on, as well as noting down the general location, time of day you managed to see the species, and so on. Use the panel for sketches as well as notes, if you come across a butterfly that stays in one place for long enough for you to try to capture it on paper.

Opening hours and admission

When given, the times of opening and the admission fees for sites were correct at time of going to press. However, admission fees are reviewed from time to time so you may find that they have been slightly increased.

How to read the maps

Distribution maps for butterflies in the field guide section of the book show whether each species is a resident or migrant, and where it is likely to be seen. Where you see a butterfly and the time of year can be useful clues to its identity.

Green tints on the maps show the areas where resident species breed in Britain. Red tints show the areas where regular migrants are likely to be seen. Pink tints show the areas where irregular migrants are likely to be seen.

The summer range of migrant butterflies is less precise than the breeding range of residents. The range of migrants given in the maps indicates the areas where they are most likely to be seen, depending on whether they arrive from the south, south-east, south-west, east or west. Of course, some migrants and some home-reared and released butterflies may occasionally be found outside the usual range for the species. Britain has 62 species of butterfly, 54 of them residents which breed here and eight either regular or irregular immigrants. Most migrant butterflies fly westwards and northwards from central and southern Europe and North Africa in early summer, reaching Britain within a few weeks.

There is rarely a return migration in the autumn as the adult insects have a life of only about 6 weeks, and the eggs, caterpillars or chrysalises that they leave behind them die when winter arrives. The monarch butterfly is the only migrant which reaches Britain from across the Atlantic, accidentally blown across by gales.

The large map on page 96 gives the approximate location of the properties mentioned in the gazetteer which follows it. More precise reference to the location of the sites can be found in the entries.

Butterfly families

Skippers

A lively habit of flitting from flower to flower and darting off to chase away other insects has led to the family name of 'skipper'. These are small, compact butterflies which fly with great speed and manoeuvrability. The ratio of the wing to the rest of the body is quite different from that of other butterflies. The wings and the body are proportionately much longer. The skipper's head is also unusual in being the same width as the thorax with large compound eyes for all-round vision at high speed. The fore-wings are highly flexible; they can not only be raised and lowered during flight but can be drawn backwards, like a swing-wing aircraft. Small, large and Essex skippers hold their wings when resting in a characteristic manner − the fore-wing partially raised and the hind-wing horizontal − which probably helps the skipper to absorb the sun's warmth, heating the butterfly's naturally cold blood and giving it energy. The dingy skipper, however, rests like a moth with wings flat on the abdomen.

Skippers are often aggressive in defence of a patch of grass or wild flower. Using tall plants or grass stems as look-out posts they will make sudden sorties to intercept passing insects, including other skippers, flies and bumble-bees. The skipper caterpillars all feed inside a curled leaf or in a protective tent of several leaves drawn together with silk. This structure may also serve the caterpillar as a safe place, or hibernaculum, during the winter. One adaptation to this sheltered way of life is that the caterpillar has a comb-like flap which propels its droppings away from the feeding area.

The Whites and Yellows

The British Pieridae family contains two major sub-families − the whites (Pierinae) and the yellows (Coliadinae) and a third sub-family (Dismorphiinae) of which the wood white is the only British member. All species in the family contain white or yellow pigments. Their eggs are tall and ribbed, and the caterpillars do not have spines. The caterpillars' food plants are mostly in the cabbage and pea families, but the brimstone caterpillar feeds solely on buckthorn. The brimstone is the only one of the British whites and yellows to hibernate as a butterfly: most of the others hibernate as chrysalises.

The white and yellow colours of the white sub-family are caused by waste products stored in the wings and the black marks they display are chemically similar to the pigments that tan human skin. Variations in colour depend on the season − butterflies of the spring generation tend to have heavy black marks. The black-and-white markings serve as a warning to predators. Birds soon learn that these insects contain poisons − mustard oil glycosides − which the butterflies obtain from cabbage leaves.

Recognising whites

Among the whites there are six different types of butterfly that look almost identical at a glance, but recognition can be greatly helped by the location in which they are seen and the time of year. White butterflies in a garden, especially where cabbages are growing, are likely to be either small or large white. The first to appear in the season will be small white, as large whites do not appear until late April. Waysides where wild flowers grow − particularly cuckoo flower and garlic mustard − are likely haunts for orange tips. Damp fields and ditches attract the green-veined white. The smallest species, the wood white, is likely to be seen only in open areas of conifer plantations.

The Aristocrat butterflies

Early entomologists devised the term 'aristocrats' for the largest and most colourful butterflies in the British countryside which they gave noble-sounding names such as purple emperor, red admiral and painted lady. The aristocrats, together with the fritillaries, make up the large family of British butterflies known as nymphalids. The nymphalids are also called brush-footed butterflies as their short, non-functional front pair of legs are held forward, close to the head, and are covered with long hairs. Consequently, they all appear to have only four legs instead of six. Most of the aristocrats live through the winter as hibernating butterflies, but the red admiral, painted lady and Camberwell beauty are not normally able to survive the British winter, and they migrate to the British Isles from the continent of North Africa each year.

The stinging nettle has been adopted by several aristocrats as their food plant. One of Britain's best known butterflies, the small tortoiseshell, lays its eggs on the stinging nettle, and its dark, spiny caterpillars can be seen eating the leaves in spring and summer. However, the large tortoiseshell, which lays its eggs on elm and other trees is now rare, partly because of the loss of 25 million elm trees from Dutch elm disease since 1970.

The sexes of the aristocrats are not easy to tell apart by colour alone, except for the purple emperor, whose female lacks the purple in the wings. The females of the peacock and white admiral are distinguishable only by being slightly larger than the males.

The Fritillaries

The word fritillary is the name of both a spotted plant − the snake's head fritillary − and a group of spotted butteflies which, together with the aristocrats, make up the Nymphalidae family. The word fritillary comes from the latin *fritillus*, meaning dice box. It may originally have been used to describe the chequer pattern on the flower in the mistaken belief that *fritillus* also meant chessboard. Both the snake's head fritillary (flower) and the heath fritillary (butterfly) are now endangered species in Britain.

Fritillaries vary greatly in the spotted pattern on their wings and in their background colour. This can create difficulty in distinguishing one species from the other, although males and females are fairly easy to recognise in most species as the females are larger, lighter-coloured and have rounded wingtips.

Most of the British fritillaries live in open sections of woodland – glades, rides, clearings and woodland margins. Six species are dependent for their caterpillars' food on woodland violets: dark green fritillary, Queen of Spain fritillary, silver-washed fritillary, high brown fritillary, the pearl-bordered and the small pearl-bordered fritillary. Populations of fritillaries in Britain have suffered dramatically since the early 1960s, as woods and scrubland have been cleared for farming and deciduous woods have been replaced by conifer plantations. The sight of large orange-brown fritillaries flying through woodland clearings in south-east England is now only a memory in many places.

Although the Duke of Burgundy fritillary shares the fritillaries' colour and name, is it not, in fact, one of the Nymphalidae family. It is the only British member of the Riodinidae family.

Blues, Hairstreaks and Copper

The Lycaenidae family of butterflies includes the blues, the hairstreaks and Britain's only copper. They are all small butterflies and mostly swift flyers. The blues and the copper have bright metallic colours while the hairstreaks have more modest colours, usually with a fine white line on the underside of the wings, from which they take the name 'hairstreak'. The blues and small copper are found in open grassy areas rich in wild flowers, while the hairstreaks, particularly the purple, black and brown hairstreaks, occur in woodlands and glades.

Caterpillars of the white-letter hairstreak, the green hairstreak, the silver-studded blue and the chalk-hill blue all have a 'honey-gland' on their bodies which secretes a fluid that ants like to drink. In return for the caterpillar's secretion, the ants probably help to keep away predatory bugs, flies and wasps. Ants are known to 'farm' caterpillars, moving them to suitable food plants in return for the secretion – a good example of symbiosis in the insect world. The large blue, for example, forms this kind of partnership with one particular species of ant, *Myrmica sabuleti*.

Browns

The brown butterflies, or Satyridae family, all have false eyes on the upper or lower surface of the wing. These eyes confuse predatory birds or lizards about the position of the body, giving the butterfly a greater chance of surviving the attack. All but one of the brown family are in fact coloured brown; the odd one out is the marbled white which is black with white markings. The browns, like the aristocrats and the fritillaries, have only four walking legs. The caterpillars of browns all eat grass, and all species spend the winter as caterpillars, feeding during the mild weather. The speckled wood may also live through the winter as a chrysalis. Members of the brown family can be found all over Britain. Three of the 11 species – the large heath, the mountain ringlet and the Scotch argus – occur almost exclusively in the north. The gatekeeper and marbled white are predominantly southern.

Butterfly names

The scientific name of each butterfly consists of two words. The second word indicates the species, a group of identical insects that can be interbreed. The first name indicates the genus, a group of closely related insects, usually with obvious similarities. The small blue butterfly, for example, is called *Cupido minimus*, from the Roman god of love and the butterfly's small size. *Cupido* is the genus, and *minimus* is the species within the genus.

When one genus closely resembles another, they are grouped together into a family. Blue butterflies share similar characteristics of wing shape and metallic colour with hairstreaks and coppers, and so all belong to the family Lycaenidae.

The eight families of butterflies are all grouped into the insect order Lepidoptera (meaning 'scaly wings') which also includes moths. All the orders of insects together make up the zoological class Insecta.

Identifying caterpillars by their food plant

When you are attempting to name a particular butterfly's caterpillar, try also to identify the plant it is eating. Some caterpillars have only one food plant; others have several; but the plant is always a good guide. The number of legs is another crucial point of identification. The caterpillars of butterflies (and moths) usually have four pairs of prolegs, the sucker-like false legs in the centre of the body. If there are more than four pairs, it is not likely to be a butterfly caterpillar.

Butterfly groups	Species	Caterpillar's principal food plants
SKIPPERS Hesperiidae	small skipper	grass
	Essex skipper	grass
	large skipper	cock's-foot grass, false brome grass
	Lulworth	chalk false brome grass, couch grass
	silver-spotted skipper	sheeps's-fescue grass, tufted-hair grass
	chequered	upright brome grass, tor grass
	dingy skipper	bird's-foot trefoil
	grizzled skipper	wild strawberry, brambles, creeping cinquefoil and wild raspberry
WHITES AND YELLOWS Pieridae *Sub-families:* Pierinae *(whites)* Dismorphiinae *(wood white)* *and* Coliadinae *(yellows)*	large white	wild and cultivated cabbage
	small white	wild and cultivated cabbage
	green-veined white	wild cabbage
	wood white	bitter vetch, bird's-foot trefoil
	brimstone	buckthorn, elder buckthorn
	orange tip	creeping yellow cress, cuckoo flower, large bittercress, wild turnip, garlic mustard
	clouded yellow	clover, lucerne, bird's-foot trefoil
	pale clouded yellow	clover, lucerne
	Berger's clouded yellow	horseshoe vetch, crown vetch
ARISTOCRATS Nymphalidae	small tortoiseshell	stinging nettle
	large tortoiseshell	elm, sallow, willow, cherry
	purple emperor	sallow
	peacock	stinging nettle
	painted lady	thistle, burdock, mallow, stinging nettle
	Camberwell Beauty	*does not breed in this country*
	comma	nettle, hop vines
	red admiral	nettle, hop vines, pellitory
	white admiral	honeysuckle

Butterfly groups	Species	Caterpillar's principal food plants
FRITILLARIES Nymphalidae	heath fritillary	cow-wheat
	marsh fritillary	devil's bit scabious, plantain, fox-glove, wood sage, honeysuckle
	pearl-bordered fritillary	woodland violet
	small pearl-bordered fritillary	woodland violet
	dark green fritillary	dog violet
	silver-washed fritillary	dog violet
	Queen of Spain fritillary	violets, borage, sainfoin
	Glanville fritillary	sea plantain, rib-wort plantain
	high brown fritillary	dog violet, sweet violet
Riodinidae	Duke of Burgundy fritillary	primrose, cowslip
BLUES, HAIRSTREAKS AND COPPER Lycaenidae	common blue	bird's-foot trefoil, restharrow, clover
	silver studded	gorse, bird's-foot trefoil, heather
	chalk-hill blue	horseshoe vetch
	Adonis blue	horseshoe vetch
	Short-tailed blue	bird's-foot trefoil, medick
	long-tailed blue	wild and cultivated peas
	small blue	kidney vetch
	large blue	thyme
	brown argus	rock rose, common stork's-bill
	northern brown argus	rock rose
	holly blue	holly, ivy
	black hairstreak	sloe (blackthorn)
	brown hairstreak	sloe (blackthorn)
	green hairstreak	gorse, broom, bramble
	purple hairstreak	oak, sallow, sweet chestnut
	white-letter hairstreak	wych elm, common elm
	small copper	sorrel, dock
BROWNS Satyridae	meadow brown	grasses
	gatekeeper	meadow grass, couch grass
	small heath	grasses
	large heath	sedges, fescues, cottongrass
	ringlet	grasses
	Scotch argus	grasses
	small mountain ringlet	mat-grass
	wall brown	grasses
	speckled wood	grasses including couch grass, cock's-foot
	marbled white	grasses
	grayling	grasses
INDIVIDUALS	monarch	milkweed
	swallowtail	milk parsley

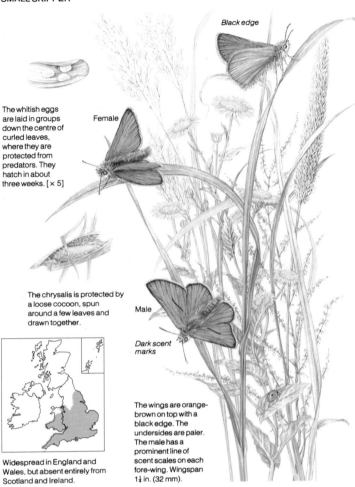

Black edge

The whitish eggs are laid in groups down the centre of curled leaves, where they are protected from predators. They hatch in about three weeks. [× 5]

Female

The young caterpillar passes the winter in a small silken cocoon, or hibernaculum.

In spring the caterpillar spends its time eating grass. It carefully protects itself from predators by pulling together the sides of a grass leaf.

The chrysalis is protected by a loose cocoon, spun around a few leaves and drawn together.

Male

Dark scent marks

Widespread in England and Wales, but absent entirely from Scotland and Ireland.

The wings are orange-brown on top with a black edge. The undersides are paler. The male has a prominent line of scent scales on each fore-wing. Wingspan 1¼ in. (32 mm).

SITES GUIDE

The green caterpillar of the small skipper may be found on grasses at any time of the year, except July, and is often seen on urban waste sites and gardens as well as in more rural locations. Small skippers may be seen at most sites in southern Britain.

Small skipper *Thymelicus sylvestris*

In July and August small skippers will be seen darting among flowers in grassy meadows in company with their close relatives the Essex skippers. The two butterflies are almost identical, except for the antennae (see Essex skipper opposite). Large skippers may also be found in the same meadow but they are bigger, bulkier and darker than the other two species.

Small skippers favour long grass with plenty of wild flowers. They drink the nectar of the flowers, particularly scabious, mayweeds, dandelions, fleabane, thistles and knapweeds. And they lay their eggs on grasses such as Yorkshire fog, soft grass, Timothy, and wood false brome, which the caterpillars will eat when they hatch. The butterflies also use the tall grasses and flowers as vantage points from which to conduct sorties against other insects that trespass on their territory.

Small skippers are alert little butterflies which live for about 20 days. They are difficult to follow in flight as they dart about at great speed. When they are resting they sometimes hold their hind-wings slightly backwards – like a swing-wing aircraft – and sometimes incline their fore-wings upwards. The attitudes are unmistakable characteristics of the skippers.

Notes and Sketches

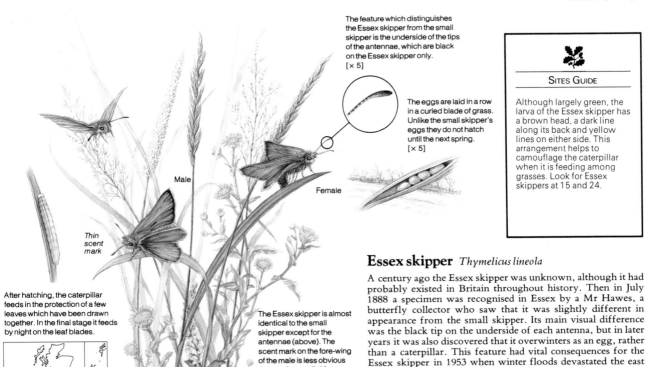

The feature which distinguishes the Essex skipper from the small skipper is the underside of the tips of the antennae, which are black on the Essex skipper only. [× 5]

The eggs are laid in a row in a curled blade of grass. Unlike the small skipper's eggs they do not hatch until the next spring. [× 5]

Male

Female

Thin scent mark

After hatching, the caterpillar feeds in the protection of a few leaves which have been drawn together. In the final stage it feeds by night on the leaf blades.

Found only in England, principally in East Anglia and the south-east.

The Essex skipper is almost identical to the small skipper except for the antennae (above). The scent mark on the fore-wing of the male is less obvious than on the small skipper. Wingspan 1⅛ in. (28 mm).

The chrysalis is protected in a coarse cocoon which is spun around a few leaves and debris near the ground.

SITES GUIDE

Although largely green, the larva of the Essex skipper has a brown head, a dark line along its back and yellow lines on either side. This arrangement helps to camouflage the caterpillar when it is feeding among grasses. Look for Essex skippers at 15 and 24.

Essex skipper *Thymelicus lineola*

A century ago the Essex skipper was unknown, although it had probably existed in Britain throughout history. Then in July 1888 a specimen was recognised in Essex by a Mr Hawes, a butterfly collector who saw that it was slightly different in appearance from the small skipper. Its main visual difference was the black tip on the underside of each antenna, but in later years it was also discovered that it overwinters as an egg, rather than a caterpillar. This feature had vital consequences for the Essex skipper in 1953 when winter floods devastated the east coast of Essex and Kent where its population is at its densest. Many eggs of the Essex skipper survived the flood waters while the caterpillars of other butterflies died in great numbers.

The Essex skipper is found over a wide area of south-east England, particularly along the Thames estuary as far upstream as the eastern suburbs of London. These quick-flying butterflies occur in the same areas of long grass as the small skippers, including motorway verges and coastal embankments. They can also be found on grassy areas of heath and downland, and along forestry rides or on farms. They feed on the nectar of many wild flowers, and the caterpillars live on grass.

Notes and Sketches

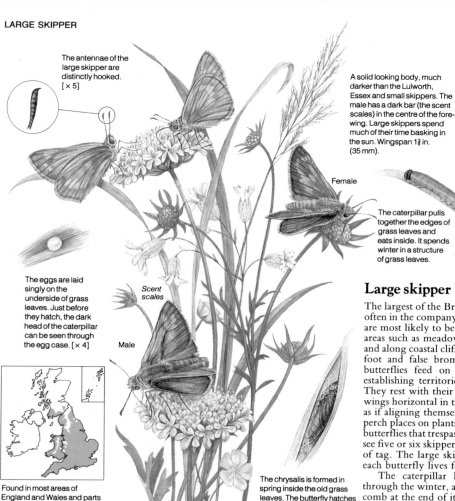

The antennae of the large skipper are distinctly hooked. [× 5]

A solid looking body, much darker than the Lulworth, Essex and small skippers. The male has a dark bar (the scent scales) in the centre of the fore-wing. Large skippers spend much of their time basking in the sun. Wingspan 1⅜ in. (35 mm).

Female

SITES GUIDE

The large skipper is not only common in England and Wales, it also occurs throughout Europe and from northern Asia to China and Japan. In warmer climates, these butterflies have up to three broods a year. Large skippers are widespread and may be seen at most of the English and Welsh sites in this book.

The caterpillar pulls together the edges of grass leaves and eats inside. It spends winter in a structure of grass leaves.

The eggs are laid singly on the underside of grass leaves. Just before they hatch, the dark head of the caterpillar can be seen through the egg case. [× 4]

Scent scales

Male

Found in most areas of England and Wales and parts of southern Scotland.

The chrysalis is formed in spring inside the old grass leaves. The butterfly hatches three weeks later.

Large skipper *Ochlodes venata*

The largest of the British skippers is found throughout England, often in the company of small and Essex skippers. Large skippers are most likely to be seen from early June to mid-July in grassy areas such as meadows, hillsides, paths and clearings in woods, and along coastal cliffs. The caterpillar's two food plants, cock's-foot and false brome grass, are widespread in Britain. The butterflies feed on flowers, but spend most of their time establishing territories, finding mates and basking in the sun. They rest with their fore-wings partially raised and their hind-wings horizontal in the typical skipper manner and fidget about as if aligning themselves to the sun's rays. They have favourite perch places on plants, from which they sally out to engage rival butterflies that trespass on their territories. It is a common sight to see five or six skippers in hot pursuit of each other as if in a game of tag. The large skipper produces one generation a year, and each butterfly lives for about three weeks.

The caterpillar lives for about 11 months, hibernating through the winter, and has one unusual feature – an 18-toothed comb at the end of its abdomen which flicks its droppings well away from the area where it is feeding.

Notes and Sketches

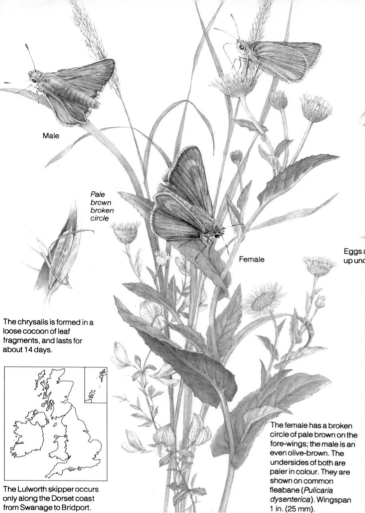

Male

Pale
brown
broken
circle

Female

The chrysalis is formed in a
loose cocoon of leaf
fragments, and lasts for
about 14 days.

The Lulworth skipper occurs
only along the Dorset coast
from Swanage to Bridport.

The female has a broken
circle of pale brown on the
fore-wings; the male is an
even olive-brown. The
undersides of both are
paler in colour. They are
shown on common
fleabane (*Pulicaria
dysenterica*). Wingspan
1 in. (25 mm).

When it emerges, the
caterpillar eats the
nutritious egg case and
then hibernates until the
following spring when it
begins feeding on grass.

Eggs are laid in rows along the curled-
up underside of a grass leaf. [× 4]

SITES GUIDE

The caterpillar of this
butterfly is another of the
grass feeders. It hibernates
soon after hatching to wait
for spring to continue its
development. It is mostly
restricted to Dorset where it
can be locally abundant.

Lulworth skipper *Thymelicus acteon*

The butterfly is named after Lulworth Cove in Dorset where it
was discovered in 1832. It has never been recorded in any
numbers out of the coastal area between Swanage and Bridport.
But where this small butterfly does occur it can be very numerous. An entomologist who studied Lulworth skippers in the
Purbeck Hills before the First World War wrote of them
'swarming up the precipitous slopes of Corfe Castle'.

The Lulworth skipper prefers warm, south–facing slopes on
the coastal cliffs. The caterpillar feeds on two species of
grass–chalk false brome and couch grass. Some of the Lulworth
Cove area is owned by the Ministry of Defence, so the butterfly
is probably prospering better than if its breeding grounds were
crowded with holiday-makers in summer.

The Lulworth skipper is a little dull to look at and could be
confused with the small skipper. It rests in the typical skipper
attitude (see opposite) and is fond of wild flowers such as
restharrow, cow parsley, ragwort, marjoram and thistles. Like
other skippers, it is a powerful flyer. There is one generation a
year – between July and August – and each butterfly lives for
about three weeks.

Notes and Sketches

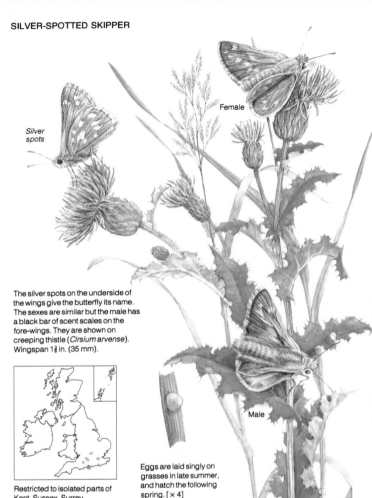

Silver spots

Female

The silver spots on the underside of the wings give the butterfly its name. The sexes are similar but the male has a black bar of scent scales on the fore-wings. They are shown on creeping thistle (*Cirsium arvense*). Wingspan 1⅜ in. (35 mm).

Restricted to isolated parts of Kent, Sussex, Surrey, Hampshire and Dorset.

Male

Eggs are laid singly on grasses in late summer, and hatch the following spring. [× 4]

The chrysalis is formed in a substantial cocoon of pieces of grass and soil at ground level. The butterfly hatches in August.

When freshly hatched the caterpillar is bright yellow, but later becomes dark with a distinctive black head.

Sites Guide

The larva of this fine butterfly has a black head and an olive-buff body and is a grass feeder. The adults eat low-growing thistles, some of which, like the carline thistle, are restricted in the areas in which they grow and tend to limit the spread of these insects. Sites for this species have not been recorded in this book.

Silver-spotted skipper *Hesperia comma*

These active little butterflies are found on open chalk grassland containing a mixture of wild flowers and grasses. The caterpillars eat sheep's-fescue grass and tufted hair-grass. The butterflies feed on flowers growing low down, such as stemless and carline thistles, hawkbits and clovers.

Distribution maps of the silver-spotted skipper published at the end of the Second World War showed a clear outline of the Chilterns and the South and North Downs. Today the butterfly has contracted to isolated pockets along these chalky corridors. Its decline has been brought about by the loss of suitable habitats. Old chalk pastures have been ploughed up, new crops such as oil-seed rape have replaced fields of clover, and areas of grassland have been given over to forestry. The loss of rabbits from myxomatosis may have resulted in other areas becoming overgrown with scrub.

Silver-spotted skippers are easily confused with the large and small skippers which may be flying in the same area. The silver spots on the undersides are the main distinguishing features. They are alert insects, and often rest with wings slanted backwards and antennae forwards, ready to chase off other insects.

Notes and Sketches

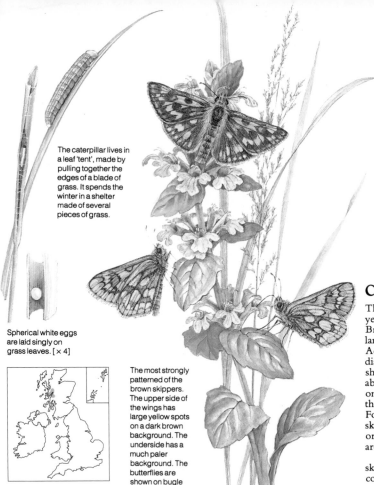

The caterpillar lives in a leaf 'tent', made by pulling together the edges of a blade of grass. It spends the winter in a shelter made of several pieces of grass.

The chrysalis is spun on to a dried leaf, and enclosed in a small cocoon.

Spherical white eggs are laid singly on grass leaves. [× 4]

SITES GUIDE

When it first emerges, the caterpillar of the chequered skipper is a light green but, by the time it is ready to pupate, it has changed colour to a pale yellowish-brown with a dark brown head. These butterflies have not been recorded at any of the National Trust properties in this book.

Now extinct in England; survives only near the Great Glen in western Scotland.

The most strongly patterned of the brown skippers. The upper side of the wings has large yellow spots on a dark brown background. The underside has a much paler background. The butterflies are shown on bugle (*Ajuga reptans*). Wingspan 1¼ in. (32 mm).

Chequered skipper *Carterocephalus palaemon*

The chequered skipper became extinct in England in 1975, 177 years after it was discovered in Bedfordshire. It now survives in Britain only in small populations in the western Scottish highlands, and is protected by the 1981 Wildlife and Countryside Act. Before it disappeared from England, the butterfly lived in a diagonal strip of limestone countryside from Devon to Lincolnshire – the same area as the large blue (which became extinct at about the same time) and the black hairstreak. Fifty-four colonies were recorded in the east Midlands before they declined in the 1960s. One of the main English localities was Rockingham Forest, around Corby in Northamptonshire. The chequered skipper lived in clearings and rides in ancient coppice woodlands or old grasslands on chalky soils. The caterpillars' food plants are upright brome grass and tor grass.

Several factors were responsible for the loss of the chequered skipper from England. Coppices have been neglected and become overgrown. Other woodlands have been removed or turned over to pine forests. Grazing, even by rabbits, is necessary to maintain a suitable grassy habitat, and the rabbit population has been severely reduced by myxomatosis.

Notes and Sketches

The caterpillar spends much of its time out of view in a tent of leaves, where it also hibernates through the winter.

A dull brown butterfly with a grey fringe to the hind-wings. The underside of the wings is light brown with white spots, and the antennae are ringed with black and white. The only food plant, bird's-foot-trefoil (*Lotus corniculatus*), is known in coastal areas as 'bacon-and-eggs'. Wingspan 1 in. (25 mm).

The chrysalis is formed in spring, inside the caterpillar's winter quarters. The butterfly hatches a month later.

Grey fringe

White spots

Single eggs, each with 12 or 13 'keels' down the side, are laid on the leaves of the food plant. [× 4]

Mostly found in southern and central Britain. The only skipper in Ireland.

Sites Guide

The dull coloration of this butterfly enables it to enjoy basking in the sun on bare ground with its wings spread wide, without risk of falling prey to a passing bird. It turns up in a variety of places ranging from railway banks to mountain sides. Look out for it in particular at 7, 9, 10, 12, 13, 15, 17, 19, 21, 24, 40, 42, 44, 54–57, 59, 60.

Dingy skipper *Erynnis tages*

Despite the name, which reflects its dull colours, the dingy skipper has attractive mottled patterns on the wings, especially the border of grey hairs around the hind-wing. It is unique among British skippers for two reasons: it is the only skipper that is also found in Ireland, and it rests at night like a moth with its wings flat over the abdomen. In sunshine it does not assume the typical skipper stance (see p. 14), but basks with the wings spread out flat. Its distribution in Britain is rather patchy, mostly in southern and central England, parts of Wales and a few places in Scotland. In Ireland it is found in limestone areas such as Counties Clare, Mayo and Galway.

The caterpillars have only one food plant, bird's-foot-trefoil, which is found throughout the British Isles but grows best on chalk and limestone soils. Dingy skippers are most likely to be seen on chalk downlands and in flowery woodland clearings in limestone districts. Like some other skippers, they overwinter as caterpillars which turn into chrysalises in April or May. The butterflies are on the wing in May and June, each one living for about 20 days. There is normally only one generation a year, with occasionally a second in favourable years.

Notes and Sketches

At first, the caterpillar protects itself under a silk web but later feeds in a leaf 'tent' in the typical skipper manner.

Eggs are laid singly on the upper side of wild strawberry leaves. They are delicately sculptured with 20 'keels'. [× 6]

SITES GUIDE

This is one of the only two skippers in the British Isles whose caterpillars do not feed on grass. Instead they eat a range of plant species which are common on many National Trust properties. The grizzled skipper may be seen at 9, 13, 15 and 40.

A brown-and-white speckled butterfly, with evenly spaced dark patches around the edges of the wings. It can be seen in spring, often on the flowers of the lesser celandine (*Ranunculus ficaria*). Wingspan 1⅛ in. (28 mm).

Mainly in southern England and Wales. Rarely north of the Humber.

The grizzled skipper is the only British skipper that overwinters as a chrysalis. It hatches as a butterfly about May.

Grizzled skipper *Pyrgus malvae*

This conspicuous and attractive little butterfly is easy to identify with its brown-and-white markings and grey (or 'grizzled') hairs. It basks in the sun with its wings spread out flat, but in dull weather the wings are firmly closed together over its back. In flight it is so swift and darting that it may be quite difficult to follow.

The grizzled skipper is found in central and southern England in flowery meadows and on chalk downland, especially in hollows and on sheltered slopes. The caterpillar's main food plants are wild potentillas such as barren strawberry, creeping cinquefoil and silverweed. Other plants that are sometimes used for food by the caterpillars are wild strawberry and raspberry, which grow in many parts of the North and South Downs, and also brambles in scrubby lowland areas.

The butterflies are never seen in great numbers like the blues, but they can usually be found in suitable localities. There is usually only one generation a year, with the butterfly in flight during May and June. In warm years a second generation may occur, and they appear again in August. Each butterfly lives for about two weeks.

Notes and Sketches

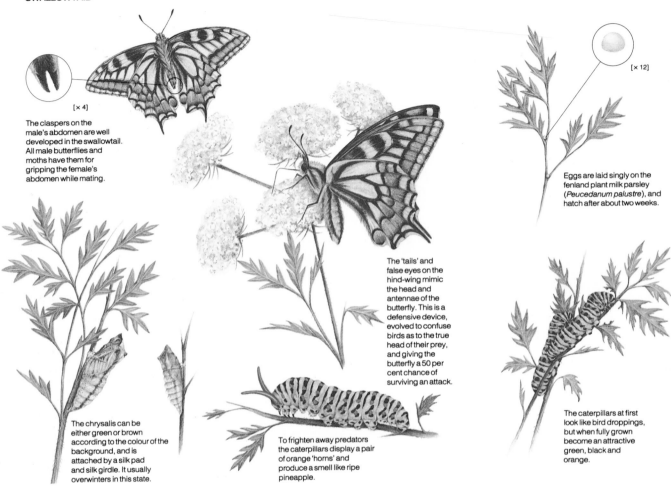

[× 4]

The claspers on the male's abdomen are well developed in the swallowtail. All male butterflies and moths have them for gripping the female's abdomen while mating.

[× 12]

Eggs are laid singly on the fenland plant milk parsley (*Peucedanum palustre*), and hatch after about two weeks.

The 'tails' and false eyes on the hind-wing mimic the head and antennae of the butterfly. This is a defensive device, evolved to confuse birds as to the true head of their prey, and giving the butterfly a 50 per cent chance of surviving an attack.

The chrysalis can be either green or brown according to the colour of the background, and is attached by a silk pad and silk girdle. It usually overwinters in this state.

To frighten away predators the caterpillars display a pair of orange 'horns' and produce a smell like ripe pineapple.

The caterpillars at first look like bird droppings, but when fully grown become an attractive green, black and orange.

Notes and Sketches

The newly emerged caterpillar has the appearance of a bird dropping to conceal it from predators – a far cry from the beautiful butterfly it will be. As it grows, it becomes green, red and black and displays two orange horns to scare off enemies. Swallowtails have not been recorded at any of the properties in this book.

Prominent 'tail'

Swallowtail butterflies are now restricted entirely to the Norfolk Broads.

This bright black-and-yellow butterfly with its red-and-blue false eyes is unmistakable. It is the largest butterfly resident in Britain, and its name refers to the extensions on the hind-wings which give the appearance of a swallow's tail. It is shown feeding on thistle flowers. Wingspan 3¾ in. (95 mm).

Swallowtail *Papilio machaon*

These lovely butterflies survive in Britain as fragile populations in a man-made habitat, the Norfolk Broads, which were excavated for peat in the Middle Ages. They are entirely dependent on the caterpillar's food plant, milk parsley, which varies in its numbers each year. The swallowtail was much more widespread in the past, occurring throughout the fens of East Anglia and probably in the marshes of the Thames and Lea rivers. It became extinct in the Wicken Sedge Fen in Cambridgeshire in the early 1950s, and an attempt was made in 1975 to reintroduce it. Conservationists planted 3,500 milk parsley plants and released 228 butterflies, but the drought of 1976 followed and the attempt failed. The butterfly is now protected by the Wildlife and Countryside Act of 1981.

Visitors to the Broads may see swallowtails from late May to mid-July. Each butterfly lives a month, but its chance of reaching the butterfly stage is small because of high losses of caterpillars and chrysalises to spiders, birds and small mammals. Land drainage was responsible for the swallowtail's disappearance in the past. Maintenance of high water levels and preservation of milk parsley are necessary for its survival in the future.

Notes and Sketches

21

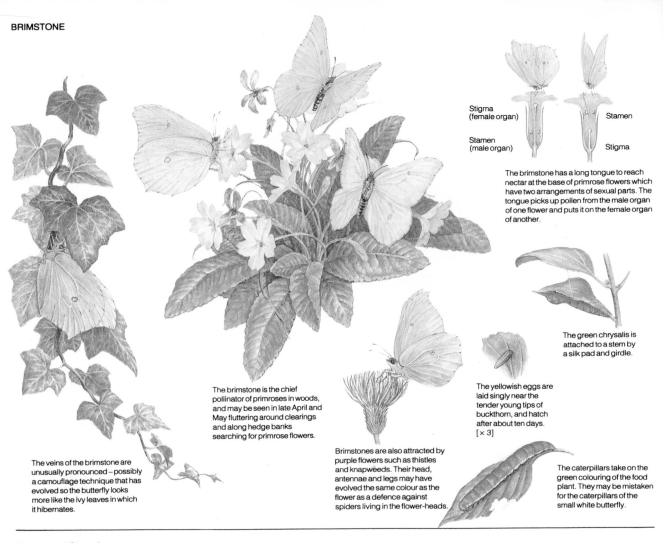

Stigma
(female organ)

Stamen

Stamen
(male organ)

Stigma

The brimstone has a long tongue to reach nectar at the base of primrose flowers which have two arrangements of sexual parts. The tongue picks up pollen from the male organ of one flower and puts it on the female organ of another.

The green chrysalis is attached to a stem by a silk pad and girdle.

The brimstone is the chief pollinator of primroses in woods, and may be seen in late April and May fluttering around clearings and along hedge banks searching for primrose flowers.

The yellowish eggs are laid singly near the tender young tips of buckthorn, and hatch after about ten days. [× 3]

The veins of the brimstone are unusually pronounced – possibly a camouflage technique that has evolved so the butterfly looks more like the ivy leaves in which it hibernates.

Brimstones are also attracted by purple flowers such as thistles and knapweeds. Their head, antennae and legs may have evolved the same colour as the flower as a defence against spiders living in the flower-heads.

The caterpillars take on the green colouring of the food plant. They may be mistaken for the caterpillars of the small white butterfly.

Notes and Sketches

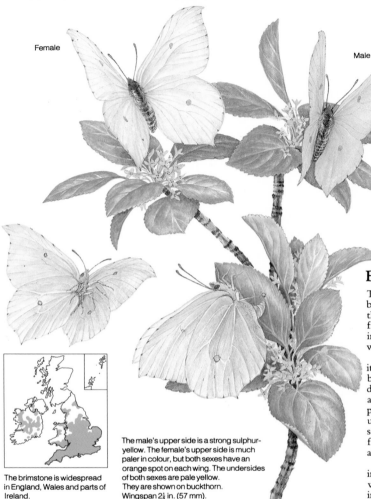

Female

Male

Orange spots

The brimstone is widespread in England, Wales and parts of Ireland.

The male's upper side is a strong sulphur-yellow. The female's upper side is much paler in colour, but both sexes have an orange spot on each wing. The undersides of both sexes are pale yellow. They are shown on buckthorn. Wingspan 2¼ in. (57 mm).

SITES GUIDE

The brimstone hibernates in ivy and the undersides of its wings match ivy leaves extremely well. As one of the earliest emergers, it is the major pollinator of woodland primroses and its long tongue is adapted to reach the nectar from these deep flowers. Brimstones are common insects and may be seen at most of the sites in southern Britain.

Brimstone *Gonepteryx rhamni*

The word butterfly was probably first used to describe this butter-coloured insect. It is a common species and is probably the first and last butterfly seen each year, as it can be in flight from February to November. 'Butterfly' eventually came to include all species and the brimstone acquired its present name which relates to the colour of sulphur.

The distribution of the brimstone mirrors the distribution of its two food plants, buckthorn (*Rhamnus catharticus*) and alder buckthorn (*Frangula alnus*), on which its caterpillars are entirely dependent for their food. The butterflies are powerful flyers and males are sometimes seen miles away from their food plants, possibly migrating to fresh territories. Brimstones are usually found on the margins of woodland, along hedgerows, in scrubby areas and thickets. They are strongly attracted to wild flowers for nectar and often stay for long periods at one flower, always with their wings shut.

The underside colours and shape allow brimstones to blend in with vegetation, and they successfully hibernate through winter as adult butterflies. There is one generation a year, and individual butterflies live for up to a year.

Notes and Sketches

Eggs are laid singly in the tight buds and flowers of a food plant. As the eggs grow older they change from greenish-white to orange.

Females prefer bluish pink and white flowers, and will occasionally visit lilac blossom in the garden.

The caterpillars are bluish-green, and are camouflaged on the long seed pods of their food plants.

Male butterflies emerge from the chrysalis before the females, and it is not unusual to see a group of males around a patch of their food plant.

The dappled green coloration of the underside provides perfect camouflage when the butterfly settles on a plant. When at rest, it moves its fore-wings backwards and inside the hind-wings.

More than 30 plants in the cabbage family have been recorded bearing eggs of the orange tip, but the caterpillars will not necessarily be successful on all of them.

Notes and Sketches

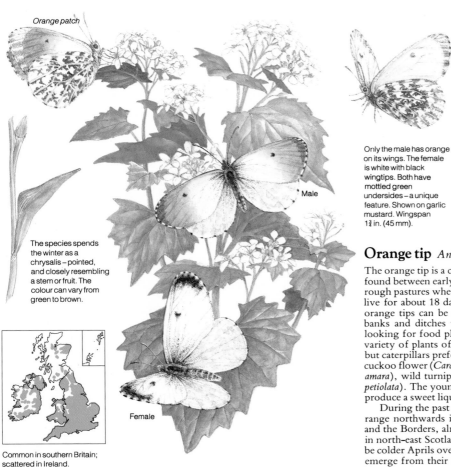

Orange patch

The species spends the winter as a chrysalis – pointed, and closely resembling a stem or fruit. The colour can vary from green to brown.

Common in southern Britain; scattered in Ireland. Spreading into Scotland.

Male

Female

Only the male has orange on its wings. The female is white with black wingtips. Both have mottled green undersides – a unique feature. Shown on garlic mustard. Wingspan 1¾ in. (45 mm).

SITES GUIDE

The male orange tip is the more prominent of the two sexes because it has bright wings. As they hatch first, the males sometimes gather at food plants where they make a fine sight. This butterfly frequents hedgerows and woodland clearings and occurs throughout the British Isles and Ireland.

Orange tip *Anthocharis cardamines*

The orange tip is a colourful symbol of spring time. It is usually found between early May and June along roadsides, ditches and rough pastures where its food plants grow. The butterflies each live for about 18 days, with only one generation a year. Male orange tips can be seen patrolling their territories along river banks and ditches while females tend to move farther afield looking for food plants where they can lay their eggs. A wide variety of plants of the cabbage family may be used for food, but caterpillars prefer creeping yellow-cress (*Rorippa sylvestris*), cuckoo flower (*Cardamine pratensis*), large bittercress (*Cardamine amara*), wild turnip (*Brassica rapa*) and garlic mustard (*Alliaria petiolata*). The young caterpillars have long forked hairs which produce a sweet liquid on which ants feed.

During the past few decades the orange tip has extended its range northwards into Yorkshire, Durham, Northumberland and the Borders, almost linking up with an isolated population in north-east Scotland. The reason for the revival is thought to be colder Aprils over the past 20 years, causing the butterflies to emerge from their chrysalises later, when more flowers are in bloom in the countryside.

Notes and Sketches

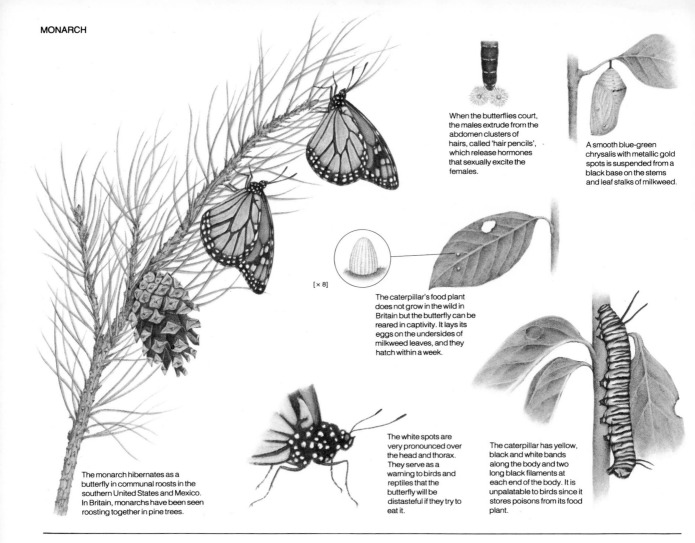

When the butterflies court, the males extrude from the abdomen clusters of hairs, called 'hair pencils', which release hormones that sexually excite the females.

A smooth blue-green chrysalis with metallic gold spots is suspended from a black base on the stems and leaf stalks of milkweed.

[× 8]

The caterpillar's food plant does not grow in the wild in Britain but the butterfly can be reared in captivity. It lays its eggs on the undersides of milkweed leaves, and they hatch within a week.

The monarch hibernates as a butterfly in communal roosts in the southern United States and Mexico. In Britain, monarchs have been seen roosting together in pine trees.

The white spots are very pronounced over the head and thorax. They serve as a warning to birds and reptiles that the butterfly will be distasteful if they try to eat it.

The caterpillar has yellow, black and white bands along the body and two long black filaments at each end of the body. It is unpalatable to birds since it stores poisons from its food plant.

Notes and Sketches

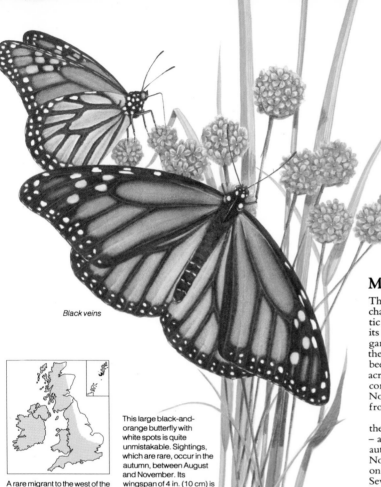

Black veins

A rare migrant to the west of the British Isles, mostly south-west England.

This large black-and-orange butterfly with white spots is quite unmistakable. Sightings, which are rare, occur in the autumn, between August and November. Its wingspan of 4 in. (10 cm) is the largest of any butterfly found in Britain.

SITES GUIDE

In its native United States, the monarch hibernates as a butterfly, roosting communally. Similar behaviour has been noted in Britain when monarchs have been seen together in pine trees. A few monarchs cross the Atlantic in the late summer and autumn and may turn up at any of the sites in the west of Ireland or the British Isles.

Monarch *Danaus plexippus*

The monarch is an American species of butterfly which, by chance, travels the vast distance of 3,500 miles across the Atlantic Ocean to Britain. It is also called the milkweed after the plant its caterpillars eat. Milkweed exists in Britain only as a very rare garden or greenhouse plant, and there is virtually no chance of the monarch breeding in this country. However monarchs have been known in Britain since 1876. They appear to be blown across the Atlantic by very strong winds, and may fly in company with the even rarer American painted lady and some North American birds. Occasionally butterflies may also arrive from the Canary Islands and Madeira.

The main migration of monarchs occurs every autumn from the northern United States and Canada to as far south as Mexico – about 1,400 miles. Those recorded in Britain are also seen in autumn – between August and October, very occasionally November. After their long sea passage they immediately feed on garden flowers, including buddleia and Michaelmas daisies. Several years may elapse between significant transatlantic crossings. A recent good year was 1981 when 140 were reported, mostly in the Isles of Scilly, Cornwall and Devon.

Notes and Sketches

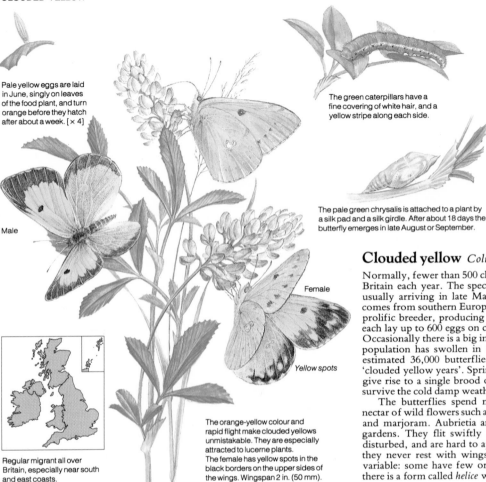

Pale yellow eggs are laid in June, singly on leaves of the food plant, and turn orange before they hatch after about a week. [× 4]

Male

Regular migrant all over Britain, especially near south and east coasts.

The green caterpillars have a fine covering of white hair, and a yellow stripe along each side.

The pale green chrysalis is attached to a plant by a silk pad and a silk girdle. After about 18 days the butterfly emerges in late August or September.

Female

Yellow spots

The orange-yellow colour and rapid flight make clouded yellows unmistakable. They are especially attracted to lucerne plants.
The female has yellow spots in the black borders on the upper sides of the wings. Wingspan 2 in. (50 mm).

SITES GUIDE

If it is a 'clouded yellow year' these butterflies should be visible at almost all of the National Trust properties recorded here, especially where food plants for the caterpillars are abundant.

Clouded yellow *Colias croceus*

Normally, fewer than 500 clouded yellow butterflies are seen in Britain each year. The species is a regular migrant to Britain, usually arriving in late May. It is a strong, fast flyer which comes from southern Europe. In its warm native countries it is a prolific breeder, producing up to four broods a year. Females each lay up to 600 eggs on clover, lucerne, trefoils and melilot. Occasionally there is a big influx into Britain after the European population has swollen in favourable conditions. In 1947 an estimated 36,000 butterflies came; 1955 and 1983 were also 'clouded yellow years'. Spring migrants to Britain lay eggs that give rise to a single brood of autumn butterflies but none can survive the cold damp weather beyond November.

The butterflies spend most of their time feeding on the nectar of wild flowers such as lucerne, clover, thistle, knapweed and marjoram. Aubrietia and marigolds may attract them to gardens. They flit swiftly from flower to flower, are easily disturbed, and are hard to approach. Always poised for flight, they never rest with wings open. The females' colouring is variable: some have few or no spots in the black margin and there is a form called *helice* which has a whitish background.

Notes and Sketches

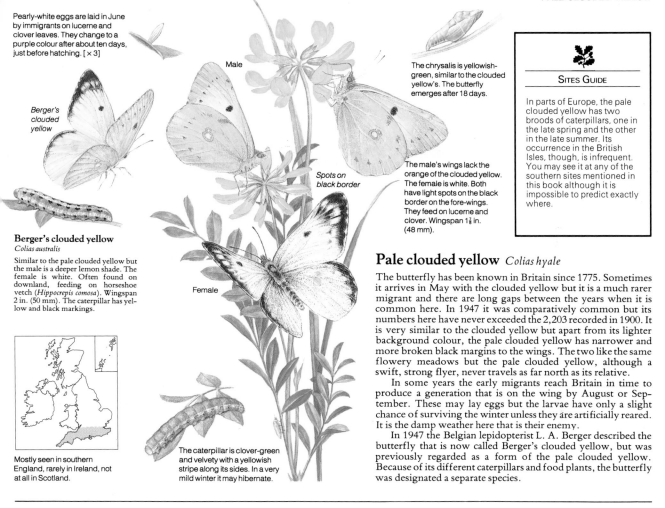

Pearly-white eggs are laid in June by immigrants on lucerne and clover leaves. They change to a purple colour after about ten days, just before hatching. [× 3]

Berger's clouded yellow

Male

The chrysalis is yellowish-green, similar to the clouded yellow's. The butterfly emerges after 18 days.

SITES GUIDE

In parts of Europe, the pale clouded yellow has two broods of caterpillars, one in the late spring and the other in the late summer. Its occurrence in the British Isles, though, is infrequent. You may see it at any of the southern sites mentioned in this book although it is impossible to predict exactly where.

Spots on black border

The male's wings lack the orange of the clouded yellow. The female is white. Both have light spots on the black border on the fore-wings. They feed on lucerne and clover. Wingspan 1⅞ in. (48 mm).

Berger's clouded yellow
Colias australis

Similar to the pale clouded yellow but the male is a deeper lemon shade. The female is white. Often found on downland, feeding on horseshoe vetch (*Hippocrepis comosa*). Wingspan 2 in. (50 mm). The caterpillar has yellow and black markings.

Female

Pale clouded yellow *Colias hyale*

The butterfly has been known in Britain since 1775. Sometimes it arrives in May with the clouded yellow but it is a much rarer migrant and there are long gaps between the years when it is common here. In 1947 it was comparatively common but its numbers here have never exceeded the 2,203 recorded in 1900. It is very similar to the clouded yellow but apart from its lighter background colour, the pale clouded yellow has narrower and more broken black margins to the wings. The two like the same flowery meadows but the pale clouded yellow, although a swift, strong flyer, never travels as far north as its relative.

In some years the early migrants reach Britain in time to produce a generation that is on the wing by August or September. These may lay eggs but the larvae have only a slight chance of surviving the winter unless they are artificially reared. It is the damp weather here that is their enemy.

In 1947 the Belgian lepidopterist L. A. Berger described the butterfly that is now called Berger's clouded yellow, but was previously regarded as a form of the pale clouded yellow. Because of its different caterpillars and food plants, the butterfly was designated a separate species.

Mostly seen in southern England, rarely in Ireland, not at all in Scotland.

The caterpillar is clover-green and velvety with a yellowish stripe along its sides. In a very mild winter it may hibernate.

Notes and Sketches

Courting butterflies respond to colour and size, chasing and spiralling with each other over meadows. As many as a dozen whites may be seen together.

Scent and sight are both necessary for a butterfly to recognise another of the correct species and sex. If a female has already mated she may raise her abdomen, refusing the male's advance.

Sensitive cells in the tips of the legs and antennae help the female to recognise the correct food plant for her caterpillars. She often lays her eggs on the underside of the leaf.

Eggs are laid in orderly groups of about 60, on leaves of the cabbage family, near the margin. As they get older, the yellow colour becomes more pronounced.

During bad weather, butterflies rest in vegetation, usually under leaves or flowers, or on grass stems. They may have to remain inactive for several days.

After a satisfactory courtship, a male and female may remain in the mating position for several hours. If disturbed, they will fly off, still joined together, with one sex carrying the passive partner below.

Notes and Sketches

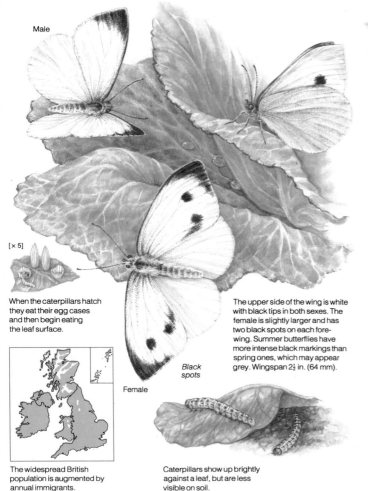

Male

[× 5]

When the caterpillars hatch
they eat their egg cases
and then begin eating
the leaf surface.

The chrysalis is found
in a sheltered spot
such as the eaves of a
shed, and may be
either green or brown.
Hibernating
chrysalises begin to
hatch in April.

The widespread British
population is augmented by
annual immigrants.

Female

Black
spots

The upper side of the wing is white
with black tips in both sexes. The
female is slightly larger and has
two black spots on each fore-
wing. Summer butterflies have
more intense black markings than
spring ones, which may appear
grey. Wingspan 2½ in. (64 mm).

Caterpillars show up brightly
against a leaf, but are less
visible on soil.

SITES GUIDE

Large whites lay their eggs in
groups of about 60 at a time,
often hiding them on the
underside of leaves. The
females are able to detect the
appropriate food plant
through sensitive cells in
their feet and antennae.
Large whites are widespread
and may be seen at most of
the sites in this book.

Large white *Pieris brassicae*

Before the 1940s, cabbage fields in Britain were often covered by
a fluttering haze of large white butterflies. The caterpillars were
major pests, destroying great numbers of cabbages. However,
the widespread use of organic insecticides since the end of the
Second World War has caused severe losses to the large whites
(as well as other butterflies), and in 1955 they were stricken by a
butterfly virus. They have never regained their previous numbers, despite regular migration of large whites from the Continent each year.

The popular name 'cabbage white' refers to both the small
and large white butterflies. Both lay their eggs on cabbages, but
the caterpillars of the large white are conspicuous and feed
exposed on the outer leaves, while the small white caterpillars
feed unseen in the heart of the cabbage. Sixty wild members of
the cabbage family are recorded as food plants, though the
caterpillars of the large white also eat garden nasturtiums and
mignonettes.

There are normally two generations of the butterfly in
Britain each year – from April to June and from July to September. The second generation have darker markings.

Notes and Sketches

31

Male

The eggs are laid singly on the underside of heart-leaves of cabbages, and hatch in a week. [× 4]

Summer chrysalises hatch in about three weeks; autumn chrysalises live through winter to produce the following year's spring generation of butterflies.

SITES GUIDE

Small whites are often seen in gardens and emerge earlier in the year than large whites, making identification easier. If the small white caterpillar has decided to pupate on a fence or wall, it will be brownish in colour rather than green like a chrysalis on a cabbage leaf. Small whites are widespread and may be seen at most of the sites in this book.

Female

Dark wingtips

The fore-wings have black tips, with one black spot on the males and two on the females. The markings on the spring generation (shown here) are paler than those on the summer generation. Wingspan up to 1⅞ in. (48 mm).

The caterpillar at first feeds in the heart of the cabbage, then later on the outer leaves.

Small whites are found all over the British Isles, including Orkney.

Small white *Artogeia rapae*

Only the meadow brown (pp. 78–79) is more common in Britain than the small white butterfly. The first generation of small whites can be seen on the wing from March to May, while the second generation flies from June to September. Their caterpillars' food plants, wild and cultivated members of the cabbage family, grow almost everywhere, so small whites are seen throughout Britain.

Although the caterpillars do less damage to the cabbage crop than large white caterpillars, they can be a more serious pest, as they are very difficult to detect. They are small and, unlike large white caterpillars, are solitary and well camouflaged by their leaf-green colouring. In addition, they start by eating the heart of a cabbage and progress gradually to the outer leaves, so that by the time they can be seen, most of the damage is done.

As the name suggests, the small white butterfly is a smaller version of the large white butterfly and, because they share a food plant and fly in the same places at similar times, they are frequently confused with each other. Apart from the difference in size, the large white has broader wings, on which the markings are usually more clearly pronounced.

Notes and Sketches

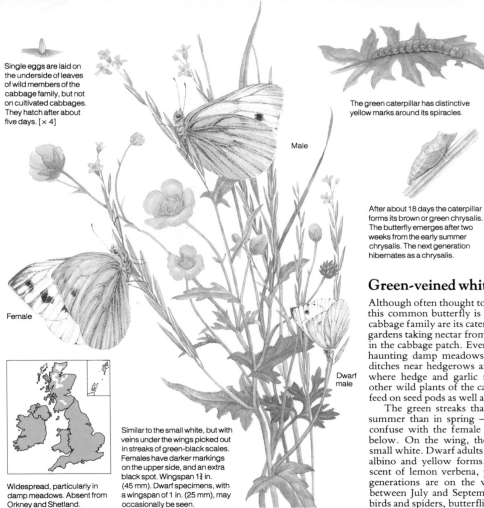

Single eggs are laid on the underside of leaves of wild members of the cabbage family, but not on cultivated cabbages. They hatch after about five days. [× 4]

Male

Female

The green caterpillar has distinctive yellow marks around its spiracles.

After about 18 days the caterpillar forms its brown or green chrysalis. The butterfly emerges after two weeks from the early summer chrysalis. The next generation hibernates as a chrysalis.

Dwarf male

Widespread, particularly in damp meadows. Absent from Orkney and Shetland.

Similar to the small white, but with veins under the wings picked out in streaks of green-black scales. Females have darker markings on the upper side, and an extra black spot. Wingspan 1¾ in. (45 mm). Dwarf specimens, with a wingspan of 1 in. (25 mm), may occasionally be seen.

Sites Guide

This is one of the few butterflies that may be seen on the wing on cloudy days although the close coloration of both the adults and the larvae to their food plants can make this a difficult butterfly to spot. Green-veined whites are widespread and may be seen at the majority of the sites in this book.

Green-veined white *Artogeia napi*

Although often thought to be a garden pest that ruins cabbages, this common butterfly is blameless; only wild relatives in the cabbage family are its caterpillars' food plants. It may be seen in gardens taking nectar from radish flowers, but it does not breed in the cabbage patch. Even on dull days the butterfly is active, haunting damp meadows, wet fields, marshy land, wayside ditches near hedgerows and woodland edges. It may be seen where hedge and garlic mustard, charlock, mignonette and other wild plants of the cabbage family grow. The caterpillars feed on seed pods as well as leaves.

The green streaks that trace the veins – more heavily in summer than in spring – make the resting butterfly easy to confuse with the female orange tip, which is green-mottled below. On the wing, the green-veined white resembles the small white. Dwarf adults are sometimes seen, and there are rare albino and yellow forms. Males exude a strong but pleasant scent of lemon verbena, probably used in courting. The two generations are on the wing between April and June, and between July and September. If they escape the attentions of birds and spiders, butterflies may live for about a month.

Notes and Sketches

33

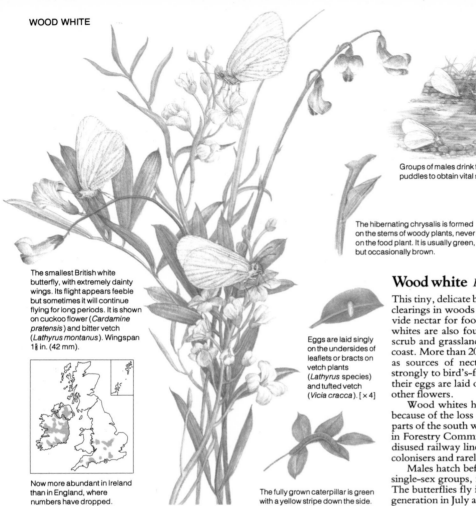

Groups of males drink from puddles to obtain vital salts.

The hibernating chrysalis is formed on the stems of woody plants, never on the food plant. It is usually green, but occasionally brown.

The smallest British white butterfly, with extremely dainty wings. Its flight appears feeble but sometimes it will continue flying for long periods. It is shown on cuckoo flower (*Cardamine pratensis*) and bitter vetch (*Lathyrus montanus*). Wingspan 1⅝ in. (42 mm).

Now more abundant in Ireland than in England, where numbers have dropped.

Eggs are laid singly on the undersides of leaflets or bracts on vetch plants (*Lathyrus* species) and tufted vetch (*Vicia cracca*). [× 4]

The fully grown caterpillar is green with a yellow stripe down the side.

SITES GUIDE

This is a frail-looking butterfly whose slow flight has meant that populations remain local. Its pupa, which is stuck to the stem of a woodland plant, looks a bit like a dead leaf to protect it against predation. This species is more common in Ireland and may be seen at 49, 51, 54−61, 62.

Wood white *Leptidea sinapis*

This tiny, delicate butterfly lives mainly along shady rides and in clearings in woods where profusely growing wild flowers provide nectar for food and suitable places for egg-laying. Wood whites are also found in sheltered meadows in Sussex and in scrub and grassland at the base of cliffs along the south Devon coast. More than 20 species of wild flowers have been identified as sources of nectar, but the butterflies are attracted most strongly to bird's-foot-trefoil, bugle and ragged robin. Most of their eggs are laid on tall food plants which stand up above the other flowers.

Wood whites have become extinct in the north of England because of the loss of their habitats. But they have prospered in parts of the south where many populations now live along rides in Forestry Commission plantations. They have also exploited disused railway lines. Because of their slow flight they are poor colonisers and rarely spread beyond limited localities.

Males hatch before females and have been seen drinking, as single-sex groups, from woodland puddles to obtain vital salts. The butterflies fly in May and June, and there may be a second generation in July and August in southern areas.

Notes and Sketches

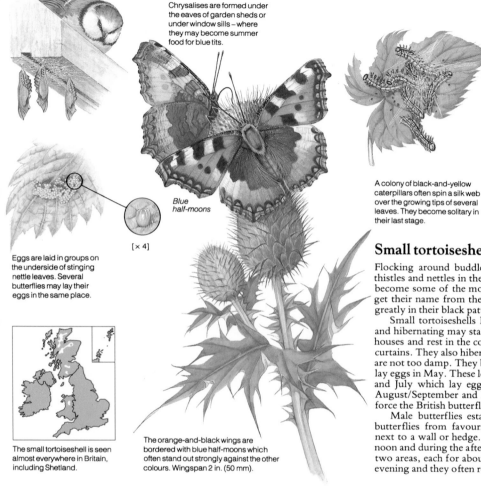

Chrysalises are formed under the eaves of garden sheds or under window sills – where they may become summer food for blue tits.

Blue half-moons

[× 4]

Eggs are laid in groups on the underside of stinging nettle leaves. Several butterflies may lay their eggs in the same place.

The small tortoiseshell is seen almost everywhere in Britain, including Shetland.

The orange-and-black wings are bordered with blue half-moons which often stand out strongly against the other colours. Wingspan 2 in. (50 mm).

A colony of black-and-yellow caterpillars often spin a silk web over the growing tips of several leaves. They become solitary in their last stage.

SITES GUIDE

At first sight, the caterpillar of this species appears to be black. This is because the black spines and black spotting conceal the true yellowy colour of the larva. The small tortoiseshell is a very common butterfly and may be seen at almost all of the sites in this book.

Small tortoiseshell *Aglais urticae*

Flocking around buddleias and ice-plants in gardens and on thistles and nettles in the countryside, small tortoiseshells have become some of the most familiar of British butterflies. They get their name from their brightly speckled wings which vary greatly in their black pattern from one to another.

Small tortoiseshells live through the winter as butterflies, and hibernating may start as early as August. They often enter houses and rest in the corners of ceilings or under pelmets and curtains. They also hibernate in garages and garden sheds which are not too damp. They become active again in mid-March, and lay eggs in May. These lead to a generation of butterflies in June and July which lay eggs to produce butterflies that hatch in August/September and live through winter. Immigrants reinforce the British butterflies in July/August.

Male butterflies establish territories by driving off other butterflies from favourite patches in sunny situations, often next to a wall or hedge. Each day they set up a territory about noon and during the afternoon each male will hold, on average, two areas, each for about 90 minutes. Mating takes place in the evening and they often roost for the night under nettle leaves.

Notes and Sketches

Most nettle-feeding caterpillars leave the nettle-patch to form their chrysalises. They often wander many yards to find a suitable place, such as fence rails, tree bark or garden sheds.

Red admiral caterpillars live alone, taking shelter in leaf-tents.

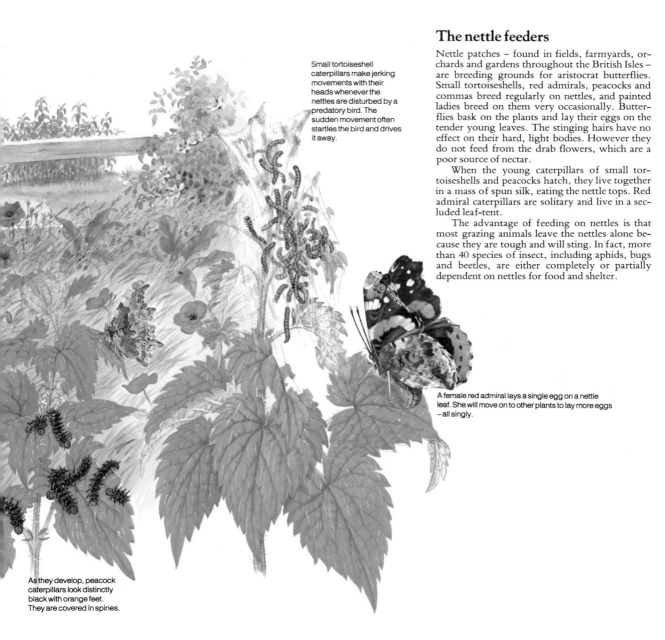

Small tortoiseshell caterpillars make jerking movements with their heads whenever the nettles are disturbed by a predatory bird. The sudden movement often startles the bird and drives it away.

The nettle feeders

Nettle patches – found in fields, farmyards, orchards and gardens throughout the British Isles – are breeding grounds for aristocrat butterflies. Small tortoiseshells, red admirals, peacocks and commas breed regularly on nettles, and painted ladies breed on them very occasionally. Butterflies bask on the plants and lay their eggs on the tender young leaves. The stinging hairs have no effect on their hard, light bodies. However they do not feed from the drab flowers, which are a poor source of nectar.

When the young caterpillars of small tortoiseshells and peacocks hatch, they live together in a mass of spun silk, eating the nettle tops. Red admiral caterpillars are solitary and live in a secluded leaf-tent.

The advantage of feeding on nettles is that most grazing animals leave the nettles alone because they are tough and will sting. In fact, more than 40 species of insect, including aphids, bugs and beetles, are either completely or partially dependent on nettles for food and shelter.

A female red admiral lays a single egg on a nettle leaf. She will move on to other plants to lay more eggs – all singly.

As they develop, peacock caterpillars look distinctly black with orange feet. They are covered in spines.

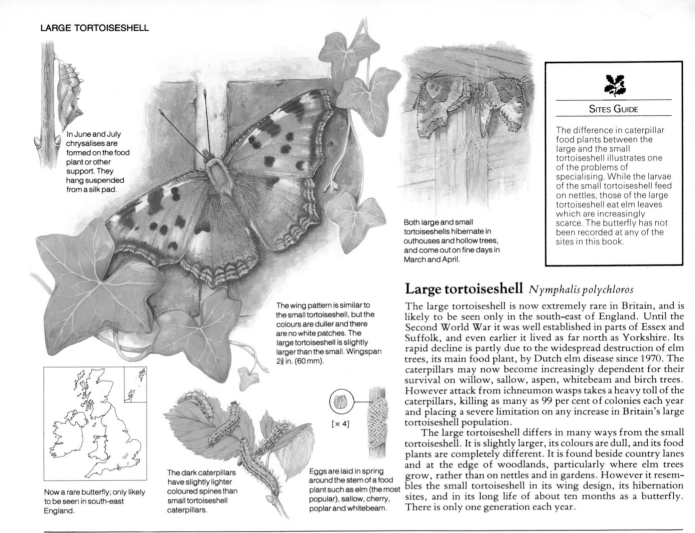

In June and July chrysalises are formed on the food plant or other support. They hang suspended from a silk pad.

Both large and small tortoiseshells hibernate in outhouses and hollow trees, and come out on fine days in March and April.

The wing pattern is similar to the small tortoiseshell, but the colours are duller and there are no white patches. The large tortoiseshell is slightly larger than the small. Wingspan 2⅜ in. (60 mm).

Now a rare butterfly; only likely to be seen in south-east England.

The dark caterpillars have slightly lighter coloured spines than small tortoiseshell caterpillars.

[× 4]

Eggs are laid in spring around the stem of a food plant such as elm (the most popular), sallow, cherry, poplar and whitebeam.

SITES GUIDE

The difference in caterpillar food plants between the large and the small tortoiseshell illustrates one of the problems of specialising. While the larvae of the small tortoiseshell feed on nettles, those of the large tortoiseshell eat elm leaves which are increasingly scarce. The butterfly has not been recorded at any of the sites in this book.

Large tortoiseshell *Nymphalis polychloros*

The large tortoiseshell is now extremely rare in Britain, and is likely to be seen only in the south-east of England. Until the Second World War it was well established in parts of Essex and Suffolk, and even earlier it lived as far north as Yorkshire. Its rapid decline is partly due to the widespread destruction of elm trees, its main food plant, by Dutch elm disease since 1970. The caterpillars may now become increasingly dependent for their survival on willow, sallow, aspen, whitebeam and birch trees. However attack from ichneumon wasps takes a heavy toll of the caterpillars, killing as many as 99 per cent of colonies each year and placing a severe limitation on any increase in Britain's large tortoiseshell population.

The large tortoiseshell differs in many ways from the small tortoiseshell. It is slightly larger, its colours are dull, and its food plants are completely different. It is found beside country lanes and at the edge of woodlands, particularly where elm trees grow, rather than on nettles and in gardens. However it resembles the small tortoiseshell in its wing design, its hibernation sites, and in its long life of about ten months as a butterfly. There is only one generation each year.

Notes and Sketches

Blue spots

Cream fringe

The dark colour of the wings, with their contrasting cream border lined with blue spots, makes the Camberwell beauty different from all other British butterflies. The undersides of the wings are similar, without the blue markings. Sexes are almost identical. Wingspan 2½ in. (64 mm).

An irregular and rare visitor, most likely to be met along the eastern side of Britain.

SITES GUIDE

While the west of the British Isles may enjoy an influx of monarch butterflies, to the east of the country, you are more likely to be the first to spot the Camberwell beauty as it flies in from Scandinavia. This butterfly is an occasional visitor and has been recorded at only one site in this book: 64.

Camberwell beauty *Nymphalis antiopa*

This exquisite butterfly, with wings like maroon velvet, was first discovered in Britain in August 1748, at the village of Camberwell, just 2 miles south of London Bridge. It was attracted to the willow trees that grew abundantly there, and took its name from the village, which later became absorbed into London. It was given various names by early entomologists, including 'white petticoat' and 'mourning cloak' after the pale hem-like fringe.

The Camberwell beauty is rarely seen, as it migrates each year from Scandinavia and has never been known to breed in this country. Hibernating butterflies probably arrive at east-coast ports on imported timber, and fly off as the weather grows warmer in the spring. Others may fly across the North Sea from Scandinavia. Camberwell beauties may be seen any time between March and August, majestically gliding around the tops of willow trees or along the streams where willows grow. They are also seen in orchards feeding on ripe fruit. They spend hours basking in the sun but, when disturbed, will dart off at great speed. They have been recorded flying over short distances at about 17 mph (26 kph).

Notes and Sketches

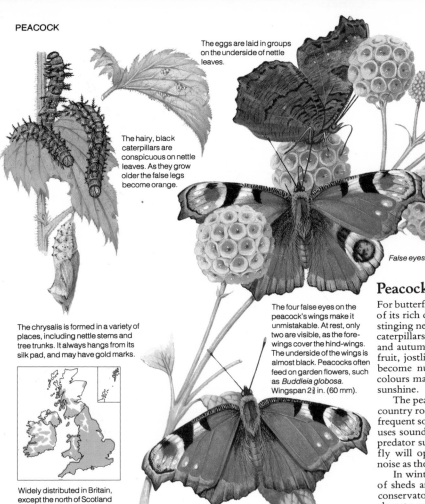

The eggs are laid in groups on the underside of nettle leaves.

The hairy, black caterpillars are conspicuous on nettle leaves. As they grow older the false legs become orange.

The chrysalis is formed in a variety of places, including nettle stems and tree trunks. It always hangs from its silk pad, and may have gold marks.

Widely distributed in Britain, except the north of Scotland and Orkney.

The four false eyes on the peacock's wings make it unmistakable. At rest, only two are visible, as the fore-wings cover the hind-wings. The underside of the wings is almost black. Peacocks often feed on garden flowers, such as *Buddleia globosa*. Wingspan 2⅜ in. (60 mm).

False eyes

SITES GUIDE

Peacocks hibernate as butterflies, often in attics and outhouses. If disturbed during the winter they may make a noise with their wings to deter predators. They are common in England and Wales and may be seen at most of the sites in this book.

Peacock *Inachis io*

For butterfly lovers, the peacock is a particular favourite because of its rich colours and its ability to live and breed in patches of stinging nettles in corners of the garden. In June the black, hairy caterpillars are easily found on the nettle leaves. In late summer and autumn the butterflies visit buddleia, ice-plants and rotten fruit, jostling for position with other butterflies. Peacocks can become numerous in orchards when the fruit ripens. Their colours make them an almost startling sight as they bask in full sunshine.

The peacock can also be found along woodland rides, beside country roads and in waste areas. It patrols its territory, making frequent sorties to investigate intruding flies and other insects. It uses sound as well as its coloured false eyes to frighten away a predator such as a bird. As the predator approaches, the butterfly will open and close its wings rapidly, making a scraping noise as the wings rub together.

In winter peacocks hibernate on the ceiling or in the corners of sheds and outhouses, and may even come into houses and conservatories looking for suitable sites. They can live for almost a year – from July until the following May.

Notes and Sketches

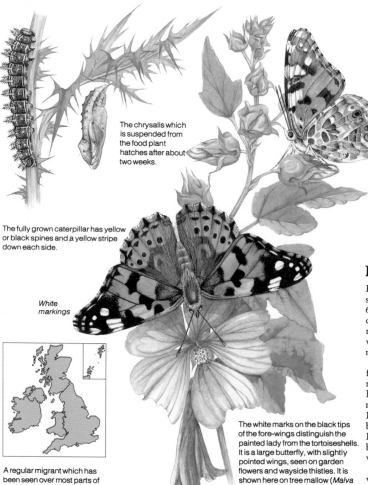

The chrysalis which is suspended from the food plant hatches after about two weeks.

The fully grown caterpillar has yellow or black spines and a yellow stripe down each side.

White markings

A regular migrant which has been seen over most parts of the British Isles.

Eggs are laid singly on the upper surface of plants including thistles, mallows, burdocks and stinging nettles.

The white marks on the black tips of the fore-wings distinguish the painted lady from the tortoiseshells. It is a large butterfly, with slightly pointed wings, seen on garden flowers and wayside thistles. It is shown here on tree mallow (*Malva arborea*). Wingspan 2¼ in. (57 mm).

SITES GUIDE

Painted ladies are apparently unable to survive European winters anywhere north of the Alps although they quickly move northwards in the spring to colonise the British Isles. They are found throughout the world except in South America. Painted ladies may be seen at most sites in the British Isles and Ireland.

Painted lady *Cynthia cardui*

Each May and June painted ladies migrate to Britain from south-west Europe and North Africa, a distance of more than 600 miles (1,000 km). In some years they are scarce, in others common. Britain was inundated with painted ladies in 1980, so many that the numbers were impossible to estimate, but there were certainly more than the 30,000 recorded in 1948. Other notable years have been 1952, 1966 and 1969.

The painted lady is a very powerful flyer. When migrating it flies at about 8 or 10 mph (13–15 kph), skimming over meadows and hedgerows. Some painted ladies reach the Shetlands and Iceland, but there is no evidence that they return in any numbers. The painted lady cannot survive the cold and humid British winter in any of its stages – egg, caterpillar, chrysalis or butterfly – but early migrants lay eggs on a wide variety of British wild flowers, giving rise to a second generation of butterflies in September and October. These die when the cold weather arrives.

When not migrating, the painted lady will settle down wherever there are flowers – perhaps on a good stand of thistles or in a garden – and devote themselves to seeking out the nectar.

Notes and Sketches

The chrysalis is formed on a sallow leaf in June or July and hatches about 18 days later.

When they hatch, the tiny caterpillars have a round, black head, but as they shed their first skins they get two distinctive 'horns' which remain with them as they develop.

Older caterpillars can be recognised by the 'horns' on the head. They hibernate when small on the exposed twigs of sallow.

Purple emperors can be seen in July and August, flying along paths in deciduous woodland. In the morning they will feed on the nectar of flowers growing along the path. By noon they fly high up into the tops of the trees where they establish territories.

Purple emperors may sometimes be seen drinking moisture from animal dung or from dead mammals such as rabbits and field mice.

The female lays her eggs singly on the upper surface of the leaves of sallow in late summer. They hatch after two weeks. [× 2]

Notes and Sketches

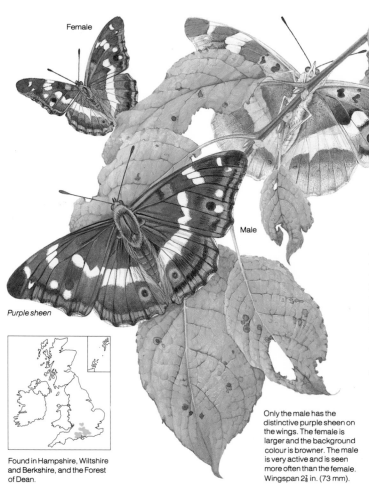

Female

Male

Purple sheen

Found in Hampshire, Wiltshire and Berkshire, and the Forest of Dean.

Only the male has the distinctive purple sheen on the wings. The female is larger and the background colour is browner. The male is very active and is seen more often than the female. Wingspan 2⅞ in. (73 mm).

SITES GUIDE

The best time to look for this butterfly is in the morning when purple emperors may be seen feeding on flowers beside rides in deciduous woodland. By midday they will be in the tree tops and almost impossible to recognise. This species has been recorded at some National Trust properties but its rarity prevents the mention of these here.

Purple emperor *Apatura iris*

This spectacular butterfly, which flies around the highest branches of oak trees, has attracted the attention of poets and tempted entomologists into lyrical description. The country poet, The Rev. George Crabbe, wrote 200 years ago: 'Above the sovereign oak, a sovereign skims, the Purple Emp'ror, strong in wing and limb.' And the 19th-century entomologist Edward Newman compared the iridescent colours of the male butterfly, which glint in woodland glades, to 'robes of Tyrian purple'. The purple emperor was given its species name *iris* after the messenger of the gods in Greek mythology who talked to mankind through the rainbow.

In the 19th century, naturalists went to extraordinary lengths to coax the butterflies from the tree-tops. They placed the rotting bodies of animals on the ground to lure them down to suck the juices. And they used nets mounted on poles up to 30 ft (9 m) long to catch them. Now the purple emperor is rarely seen. Loss of woodland, rather than the activities of collectors, has probably been the major reason for its decline. It now occurs only in parts of the New Forest and the Forest of Dean and is conserved on one Ministry of Defence site.

Notes and Sketches

The caterpillars rest in a characteristic bent shape inside their tents. There are both green and brown forms.

Single eggs are laid by spring migrants on the upper surface of nettle leaves, and occasionally on the leaves of hops and pellitory-of-the-wall.

Butterflies are on the wing from May to October. Those seen before July are migrants from the Continent.

The red admiral enjoys the juice of rotting fruit, and will compete on autumn windfalls with wasps and other butterflies, such as peacocks and commas, constantly opening and closing its wings.

The solitary caterpillars feed inside protective tents of leaves which they draw together with silk threads.

The chrysalis, which has attractive gold spots, is formed in summer and autumn, and may be seen suspended from the food plant.

Notes and Sketches

Red band

White markings

SITES GUIDE

Look out for the solitary green or brown caterpillars of this species hidden in tents of curled nettle leaves drawn together with silk threads. The chrysalis has gold spots and hangs from the food plant when formed. This is a very common butterfly and may be seen at most of the sites in this book.

Found almost everywhere in Britain – in valleys and on mountains, and in gardens.

The red bands on a black background, and white markings on the fore-wings, make the red admiral an easily recognised butterfly. It is a regular visitor to gardens, feeding on Michaelmas daisies in autumn. Wingspan 2½ in. (64 mm).

Red admiral *Vanessa atalanta*

The bright colours of the butterfly earned it the 18th-century name of the admirable, from which its modern name evolved. Its wings so resembled the robes and livery colours of noblemen and dignitaries that it was also called the alderman.

The red admiral is a familiar butterfly even though its presence in Britain depends on influxes of migrants from the Continent each year. The first butterflies start arriving in May and produce the eggs which give rise to a resident generation in the summer. It is a fast flyer which patrols small territories such as sections of hedgerows, lanes and woodland clearings, driving away intruding butterflies. It often rests and suns itself, displaying the brilliance of its outstretched wings. Unusually for a butterfly, it sometimes flies at night.

Gardeners know the red admiral as an autumn visitor to ice-plants, buddleia and Michaelmas daisies. In the wild it feeds on the nectar of teasel, scabious, clover and the flowers of ivy. It drinks water from puddles and the sap exuding from trees. And it flocks to windfall apples rotting on the ground – a scene captured by William Wordsworth in his poem *To a butterfly*: 'This plot of orchard-ground is ours.'

Notes and Sketches

With good observation, the single eggs can easily be seen on the honeysuckle leaves. A brown caterpillar hatches from the egg after about a week. [× 4]

Single eggs are laid in July, on the edge of honeysuckle leaves near the base.

In autumn, the immature caterpillar spins silken threads to anchor a honeysuckle leaf to the stem and hibernates in the withered crinkles. It resumes feeding on the new spring foliage.

In June, the mature caterpillar forms a curiously shaped, colourful chrysalis which hangs from a stem. It has metallic spots and two distinctive 'horns' on its head. The butterfly emerges after 16 days.

When fully grown, the caterpillar has a distinctive double row of branched reddish spines along its dark green body. It attaches its own droppings to itself to improve its camouflage.

Their wing-bands flicker in an oak glade as white admirals skim the honeysuckle. A male patrols the open area round a prominent tree, courting passing females and chasing away intruders.

Notes and Sketches

White band

A large, dark, woodland butterfly with a distinctive white band running across fore and hind-wings. The underside is attractively patterned. In some individuals the white band is darkened and the underside stained with black. The butterflies are shown feeding on the flowers of bramble, their favourite nectar source. Wingspan 2⅜ in. (60 mm).

Limited to southern England; mostly in Wiltshire, Dorset, Hampshire and Sussex.

SITES GUIDE

The white admiral caterpillar is unmistakable. It is found on honeysuckle leaves and is dark green with two rows of branched reddish spines down its back. To enhance its camouflage still further, it sticks its own droppings to itself. You may see this butterfly at sites 15 and 16.

White admiral *Ladoga camilla*

When this butterfly was called the white admiral in the 18th century it was an uncommon sight in the well-managed woods of England. However the mid-20th century has seen a population explosion, and the white admiral has spread out from the central counties of southern England into the West Country and Midlands. This expansion followed a series of warm summers in the 1930s and the neglect of coppice woodland where trees were once regularly trimmed and the undergrowth kept tidy. Neglect has allowed rampant growth of honeysuckle, the sole food plant of the white admiral's caterpillars.

The butterflies gather in sunny, secluded pockets of woodland throughout July. The males establish territories by making repeated powerful flights around their patch, one moment swooping low over the vegetation, the next soaring up to perch high in the trees. Solitary females flutter around honeysuckle, looking for suitable egg-laying sites. The butterflies may live for four weeks, frequently visiting clumps of brambles to drink nectar. By the end of the month their wings become torn and battered by thorns and a butterfly may end its life no longer able to take evading action from a predatory bird or dragonfly.

Notes and Sketches

47

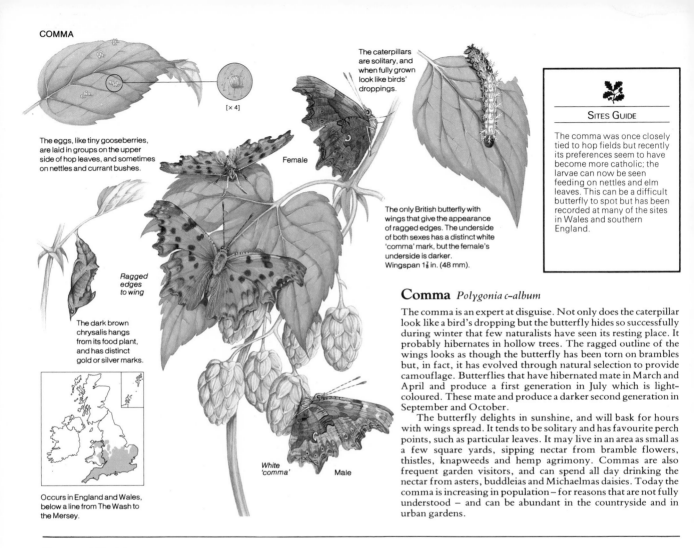

[× 4]

The eggs, like tiny gooseberries, are laid in groups on the upper side of hop leaves, and sometimes on nettles and currant bushes.

The caterpillars are solitary, and when fully grown look like birds' droppings.

Female

Ragged edges to wing

The dark brown chrysalis hangs from its food plant, and has distinct gold or silver marks.

The only British butterfly with wings that give the appearance of ragged edges. The underside of both sexes has a distinct white 'comma' mark, but the female's underside is darker.
Wingspan 1⅞ in. (48 mm).

White 'comma'

Male

Occurs in England and Wales, below a line from The Wash to the Mersey.

Sites Guide

The comma was once closely tied to hop fields but recently its preferences seem to have become more catholic; the larvae can now be seen feeding on nettles and elm leaves. This can be a difficult butterfly to spot but has been recorded at many of the sites in Wales and southern England.

Comma *Polygonia c–album*

The comma is an expert at disguise. Not only does the caterpillar look like a bird's dropping but the butterfly hides so successfully during winter that few naturalists have seen its resting place. It probably hibernates in hollow trees. The ragged outline of the wings looks as though the butterfly has been torn on brambles but, in fact, it has evolved through natural selection to provide camouflage. Butterflies that have hibernated mate in March and April and produce a first generation in July which is light-coloured. These mate and produce a darker second generation in September and October.

The butterfly delights in sunshine, and will bask for hours with wings spread. It tends to be solitary and has favourite perch points, such as particular leaves. It may live in an area as small as a few square yards, sipping nectar from bramble flowers, thistles, knapweeds and hemp agrimony. Commas are also frequent garden visitors, and can spend all day drinking the nectar from asters, buddleias and Michaelmas daisies. Today the comma is increasing in population – for reasons that are not fully understood – and can be abundant in the countryside and in urban gardens.

Notes and Sketches

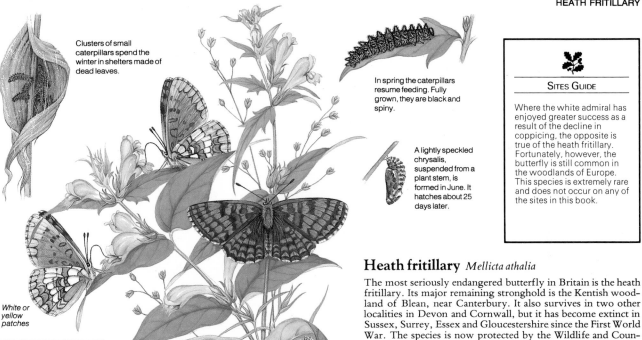

Clusters of small caterpillars spend the winter in shelters made of dead leaves.

In spring the caterpillars resume feeding. Fully grown, they are black and spiny.

A lightly speckled chrysalis, suspended from a plant stem, is formed in June. It hatches about 25 days later.

White or yellow patches

Isolated colonies of the heath fritillary exist only in Kent and the West Country.

A typical fritillary with dark orange speckled wings. The undersides of the hind-wings have large white or yellow patches. It flies in June and July, and is shown on the flowers of cow-wheat (*Melampyrum pratense*). Wingspan 1¾ in. (45 mm).

[× 4]
Groups of eggs are laid on the underside of cow-wheat leaves, and sometimes on plantain (*Plantago*).

SITES GUIDE

Where the white admiral has enjoyed greater success as a result of the decline in coppicing, the opposite is true of the heath fritillary. Fortunately, however, the butterfly is still common in the woodlands of Europe. This species is extremely rare and does not occur on any of the sites in this book.

Heath fritillary *Mellicta athalia*

The most seriously endangered butterfly in Britain is the heath fritillary. Its major remaining stronghold is the Kentish woodland of Blean, near Canterbury. It also survives in two other localities in Devon and Cornwall, but it has become extinct in Sussex, Surrey, Essex and Gloucestershire since the First World War. The species is now protected by the Wildlife and Countryside Act of 1981, but it could become extinct in Britain this century.

The butterfly thrived well in traditional coppice woodland where sweet chestnut trees were cut back to a stump every 15 years, causing new shoots to grow and providing regular crops of poles. The practice created open woodland with plenty of sunlight – ideal for the caterpillar's main food plant, cow-wheat.

Since the First World War coppicing has become increasingly uneconomic, and some areas have become overgrown and others have been ploughed up or planted with conifers. Surviving coppices are felled in very large plots, instead of the small areas of earlier years. Consequently the seeds of the food plants, and the butterflies themselves, are less able to move from one young area of coppice to another.

Notes and Sketches

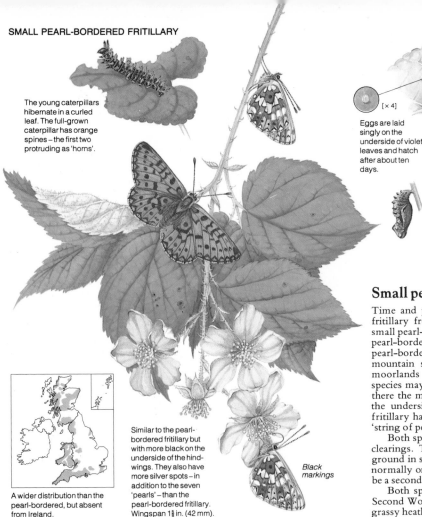

The young caterpillars hibernate in a curled leaf. The full-grown caterpillar has orange spines – the first two protruding as 'horns'.

[× 4]

Eggs are laid singly on the underside of violet leaves and hatch after about ten days.

The dark chrysalis is formed in May or June on the stem of a violet or nearby plant.

SITES GUIDE

This delightful little butterfly is sometimes found in a wide variety of habitat types, but mostly in woods. The appearance is similar to the heath fritillary but with slightly more orange spines. It has been recorded at a small number of the sites in this book although precise locations are not given.

A wider distribution than the pearl-bordered, but absent from Ireland.

Similar to the pearl-bordered fritillary but with more black on the underside of the hind-wings. They also have more silver spots – in addition to the seven 'pearls' – than the pearl-bordered fritillary. Wingspan 1⅝ in. (42 mm).

Black markings

Small pearl-bordered fritillary *Boloria selene*

Time and place help to distinguish the small pearl-bordered fritillary from the very similar pearl-bordered fritillary. The small pearl-bordered flies in June and July – a little later than the pearl-bordered which is seen in May and June. And the small pearl-bordered is found in more open areas, such as grassy mountain slopes in Wales and Scotland, together with the moorlands and moist sea-cliffs of Cornwall. However both species may be encountered in woodland clearings in June, and there the most certain means of identification is the pattern on the underside of the hind-wings. The small pearl-bordered fritillary has more pronounced silver spots – in addition to the 'string of pearls' – than the pearl-bordered.

Both species are very active, flying to and fro in glades and clearings. The small pearl-bordered flies swiftly close to the ground in search of nectar-rich flowers such as bugle. There is normally one generation a year, but in hot summers there may be a second in late August and September.

Both species have become rare in eastern Britain since the Second World War because of loss of woodlands, coppices and grassy heathlands which have become farmland or pine forests.

Notes and Sketches

Seven 'pearls' border the margins of the underside of the hind-wings. The butterfly can be distinguished from the small pearl-bordered fritillary (opposite) in having only two silver patches on the central area of the underside. It is seen in May and June. Wingspan 1¾ in. (45 mm).

Seven 'pearls'

The full-grown caterpillar, recognisable by the yellow spines, feeds on violets in spring after spending the winter in curled-up leaves.

The chrysalis, looking like a dead leaf, is formed in May. The butterfly hatches in about ten days.

Found mainly on the south and west coast of Britain and north-west Clare.

[× 3]

Eggs are laid singly on violet stems in May and June. They hatch after 10–15 days.

SITES GUIDE

Although its caterpillar is restricted to the violet, which is its food plant, this butterfly may be seen on the wing in woodlands and meadows, feeding on a variety of spring flowers. The pearl-bordered fritillary has been recorded at a small number of the sites in this book although precise reference to these is not given.

Pearl-bordered fritillary *Boloria euphrosyne*

In past centuries, spring meadows and woodland glades were filled with violets which attracted fritillary butterflies in great numbers to lay their eggs on the leaves. But the 20th century has seen meadows and glades ploughed up to grow crops. And in the meadows that remain herbicides are used to destroy plants other than grass, to give more efficient farming. Pearl-bordered fritillaries are restricted mostly to woods and coppices where violets still grow in clearings and along paths. They spend much of their time patrolling territories and visiting wild flowers such as bugles to drink the nectar. In the evenings they will bask in the setting sun, and at night they rest under the heads of grasses and rushes.

The pearl-bordered fritillary was once known as the April fritillary, but the calendar was put back by 11 days in 1752 and now it is not normally seen until May. It is very similar to its relative the small pearl-bordered fritillary (opposite). The upper sides of the wings are almost identical in the two species, and both have a 'string of pearls' decorating the underside of the hind-wings, but the pearl-bordered has fewer silver patches on the underside other than the 'pearls'.

Notes and Sketches

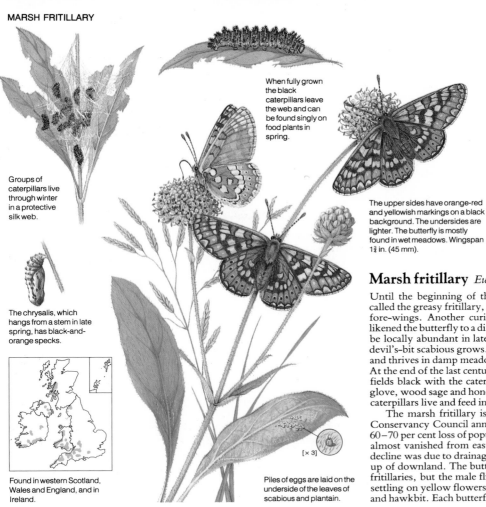

When fully grown the black caterpillars leave the web and can be found singly on food plants in spring.

Groups of caterpillars live through winter in a protective silk web.

The chrysalis, which hangs from a stem in late spring, has black-and-orange specks.

Found in western Scotland, Wales and England, and in Ireland.

The upper sides have orange-red and yellowish markings on a black background. The undersides are lighter. The butterfly is mostly found in wet meadows. Wingspan 1¾ in. (45 mm).

[× 3]

Piles of eggs are laid on the underside of the leaves of scabious and plantain.

SITES GUIDE

The marsh fritillary, in common with a number of other species, has suffered in recent years because of agricultural improvement and land drainage. This has reduced its habitat which, for such a sluggish and inactive butterfly, has been extremely harmful. The marsh fritillary can be seen at some sites in the Republic of Ireland.

Marsh fritillary *Euphydryas aurinia*

Until the beginning of this century, the marsh fritillary was called the greasy fritillary, because of the shiny undersides of the fore-wings. Another curious name was the dishclout, which likened the butterfly to a dirty dishcloth. The marsh fritillary can be locally abundant in late May and early June in places where devil's-bit scabious grows. The plant is eaten by the caterpillars, and thrives in damp meadows and wet hollows on chalk downs. At the end of the last century there were reports from Ireland of fields black with the caterpillars, which also eat plantain, foxglove, wood sage and honeysuckle. Both the butterflies and the caterpillars live and feed in groups.

The marsh fritillary is a vulnerable butterfly. The Nature Conservancy Council announced in 1981 that there had been a 60–70 per cent loss of populations of the species, which has now almost vanished from eastern England and the Midlands. The decline was due to drainage of wet meadows and the ploughing up of downland. The butterflies are not active flyers like other fritillaries, but the male flies more often than the female, often settling on yellow flowers such as dandelion, bird's-foot-trefoil and hawkbit. Each butterfly lives for about a month.

Notes and Sketches

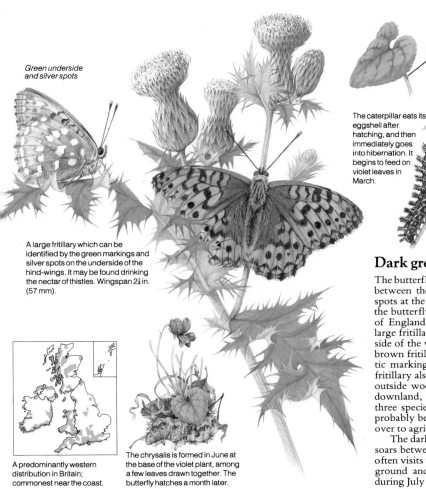

Green underside and silver spots

A large fritillary which can be identified by the green markings and silver spots on the underside of the hind-wings. It may be found drinking the nectar of thistles. Wingspan 2¼ in. (57 mm).

A predominantly western distribution in Britain; commonest near the coast.

The chrysalis is formed in June at the base of the violet plant, among a few leaves drawn together. The butterfly hatches a month later.

[×4]

Eggs are laid on leaves and stems of violets, and hatch after about 17 days.

The caterpillar eats its eggshell after hatching, and then immediately goes into hibernation. It begins to feed on violet leaves in March.

SITES GUIDE

This butterfly is on the decline in Ireland and the British Isles. The western isles of Scotland have their own sub-species – *Argynnis aglaja scotica* – which is much darker in colour. Dark green fritillaries prefer moorland and sea cliff habitats, and you may see them at the coastal sites in south-west England and south-west Wales.

Dark green fritillary *Argynnis aglaja*

The butterfly gets its name from the olive-green colour suffused between the silver spots on the underside of the wings. The spots at the base of the wing can be fused together in a form of the butterfly called *charlotta*, which was once named the Queen of England fritillary. The dark green is one of Britain's three large fritillaries and has a similar colour and pattern on the upper side of the wings as the other two – the silver-washed and high brown fritillaries. However each species has its own characteristic markings on the underside of the wings. The dark green fritillary also differs from the other two species in being found outside woods. It is more often found in open meadows and downland, woodland margins, sea-cliffs and moorlands. All three species have decreased in Britain over the past 50 years, probably because large areas of their habitats have been turned over to agriculture.

The dark green fritillary is a very fast flyer which skims and soars between flowers and between its perch-points on trees. It often visits thistles for nectar and can also be seen basking on the ground and on ferns. Each butterfly lives about six weeks during July and August.

Notes and Sketches

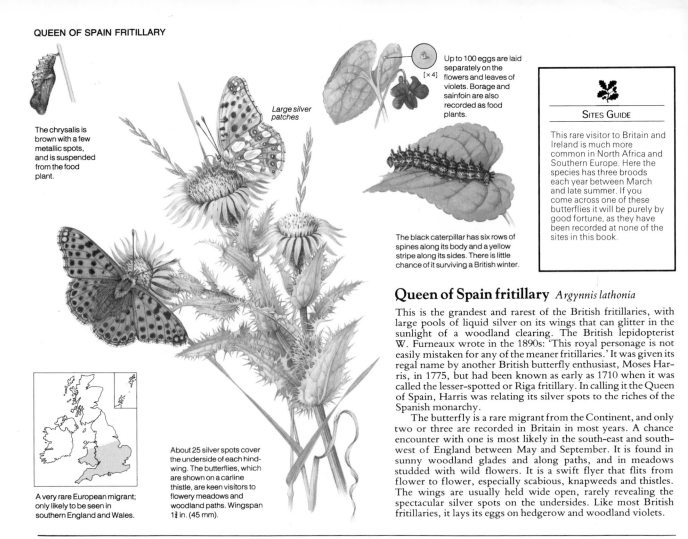

The chrysalis is brown with a few metallic spots, and is suspended from the food plant.

Large silver patches

[× 4]

Up to 100 eggs are laid separately on the flowers and leaves of violets. Borage and sainfoin are also recorded as food plants.

The black caterpillar has six rows of spines along its body and a yellow stripe along its sides. There is little chance of it surviving a British winter.

SITES GUIDE

This rare visitor to Britain and Ireland is much more common in North Africa and Southern Europe. Here the species has three broods each year between March and late summer. If you come across one of these butterflies it will be purely by good fortune, as they have been recorded at none of the sites in this book.

A very rare European migrant; only likely to be seen in southern England and Wales.

About 25 silver spots cover the underside of each hind-wing. The butterflies, which are shown on a carline thistle, are keen visitors to flowery meadows and woodland paths. Wingspan 1¾ in. (45 mm).

Queen of Spain fritillary *Argynnis lathonia*

This is the grandest and rarest of the British fritillaries, with large pools of liquid silver on its wings that can glitter in the sunlight of a woodland clearing. The British lepidopterist W. Furneaux wrote in the 1890s: 'This royal personage is not easily mistaken for any of the meaner fritillaries.' It was given its regal name by another British butterfly enthusiast, Moses Harris, in 1775, but had been known as early as 1710 when it was called the lesser-spotted or Riga fritillary. In calling it the Queen of Spain, Harris was relating its silver spots to the riches of the Spanish monarchy.

The butterfly is a rare migrant from the Continent, and only two or three are recorded in Britain in most years. A chance encounter with one is most likely in the south-east and south-west of England between May and September. It is found in sunny woodland glades and along paths, and in meadows studded with wild flowers. It is a swift flyer that flits from flower to flower, especially scabious, knapweeds and thistles. The wings are usually held wide open, rarely revealing the spectacular silver spots on the undersides. Like most British fritillaries, it lays its eggs on hedgerow and woodland violets.

Notes and Sketches

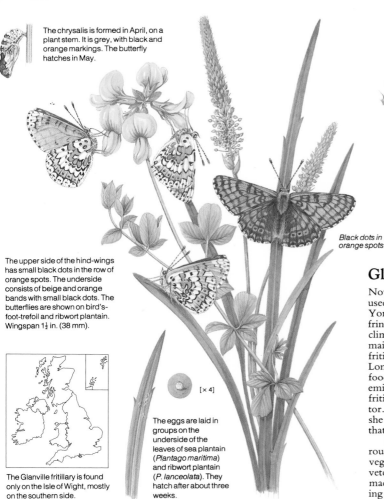

The chrysalis is formed in April, on a plant stem. It is grey, with black and orange markings. The butterfly hatches in May.

Groups of small caterpillars hibernate in a silken web until the spring. The fully grown caterpillar is black and spiny, with a distinctive reddish head.

Black dots in orange spots

The upper side of the hind-wings has small black dots in the row of orange spots. The underside consists of beige and orange bands with small black dots. The butterflies are shown on bird's-foot-trefoil and ribwort plantain. Wingspan 1½ in. (38 mm).

The Glanville fritillary is found only on the Isle of Wight, mostly on the southern side.

[× 4]

The eggs are laid in groups on the underside of the leaves of sea plantain (*Plantago maritima*) and ribwort plantain (*P. lanceolata*). They hatch after about three weeks.

SITES GUIDE

It is a pity that climatological factors have restricted the range of this butterfly in recent times for there is no shortage of ribwort plantain on which its larvae feed. Look out for these insects along the south coast of the Isle of Wight.

Glanville fritillary *Melitaea cinxia*

Now found only on the Isle of Wight, the Glanville fritillary used to be common in parts of the English mainland from Yorkshire to Wiltshire. However Britain is on the northern fringe of its range in Europe, and a barely perceptible change in climate may have been the cause of its disappearance from the mainland. The butterfly was originally called the Dullidge fritillary as it occurred in Dulwich, now a suburb of south London. Another name, the plantain fritillary, referred to the food plant of its caterpillars. Then, in the early 18th century, the eminent entomologist James Petiver named it the Glanville fritillary after Eleanor Glanville, an enthusiastic amateur collector. Mrs Glanville's will was later contested on the grounds that she was not of sound mind, her unusual hobby being regarded at that time as evidence of eccentricity.

Glanville fritillaries are sun-loving butterflies that fly on rough grassy slopes near the sea. They glide low over the vegetation, visiting yellow flowers that grow on chalk, such as vetches and trefoils, to drink their nectar. Attempts have been made in recent years to introduce them to mainland sites including the New Forest and the Wirral, so far without success.

Notes and Sketches

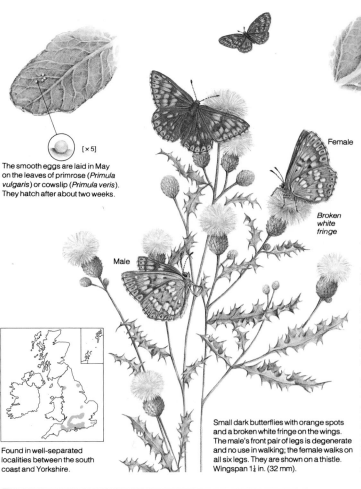

The smooth eggs are laid in May on the leaves of primrose (*Primula vulgaris*) or cowslip (*Primula veris*). They hatch after about two weeks.

[× 5]

Male

Female

Broken white fringe

The brown, hairy caterpillar feeds on the underside of the leaves.

In September a light-coloured chrysalis forms on the underside of the leaf, where it spends the winter.

Found in well-separated localities between the south coast and Yorkshire.

Small dark butterflies with orange spots and a broken white fringe on the wings. The male's front pair of legs is degenerate and no use in walking; the female walks on all six legs. They are shown on a thistle. Wingspan 1¼ in. (32 mm).

SITES GUIDE

This butterfly is not only restricted by the colder climates of the more northern areas of Europe, but its habitat is also limited by altitude. It is not found in woodlands at heights over about 3,000 feet (1,000 metres) on the continent. Duke of Burgundy fritillaries are rare and sites have not been included in this book.

Duke of Burgundy fritillary *Hamearis lucina*

Basking in the sun low down on vegetation or on bare earth is how this woodland butterfly spends most of its time. It seems to be attracted to wood spurge and blue flowers, but rarely visits other flowers for nectar. This very active flyer makes short flights between basking and often flutters over the caterpillar's food plants – primroses and cowslips. The caterpillar can be seen in the translucent greyish egg before it emerges. When fully grown, it forms a sturdy chrysalis that does not dangle but is held closely beneath a leaf by a silken girdle. The butterfly emerges in late May or June and lives about 20 days.

Although the butterfly is called a fritillary, from its resemblance to the fritillaries in pattern, it belongs to a different family – and is the only species of the family – which is chiefly South American – found in Britain. Its caterpillars do not have the honey gland, which exudes sweet fluid, as fritillary caterpillars do. It has been known as a fritillary since the 18th century when it was called Mr Vernon's small fritillary. The butterfly has never been common in Britain but it lives in many scattered localities in woodland clearings, on scrubby hillsides, and on downlands – if primroses or cowslips grow there.

Notes and Sketches

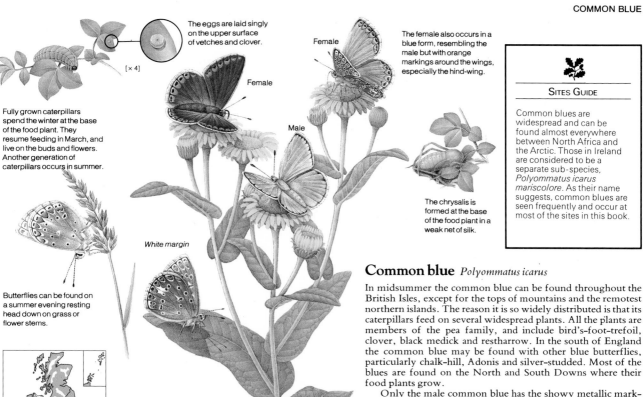

The eggs are laid singly on the upper surface of vetches and clover.

[× 4]

Female

Female

Male

White margin

The female also occurs in a blue form, resembling the male but with orange markings around the wings, especially the hind-wing.

The chrysalis is formed at the base of the food plant in a weak net of silk.

Fully grown caterpillars spend the winter at the base of the food plant. They resume feeding in March, and live on the buds and flowers. Another generation of caterpillars occurs in summer.

Butterflies can be found on a summer evening resting head down on grass or flower stems.

The common blue is found throughout the British Isles, as far north as Shetland.

The male is blue and the female usually brown with orange markings. Both have white margins around the wings. Favourite plants include fleabane, marjoram and thyme. Wingspan 1⅜ in. (35 mm).

SITES GUIDE

Common blues are widespread and can be found almost everywhere between North Africa and the Arctic. Those in Ireland are considered to be a separate sub-species, *Polyommatus icarus mariscolore*. As their name suggests, common blues are seen frequently and occur at most of the sites in this book.

Common blue *Polyommatus icarus*

In midsummer the common blue can be found throughout the British Isles, except for the tops of mountains and the remotest northern islands. The reason it is so widely distributed is that its caterpillars feed on several widespread plants. All the plants are members of the pea family, and include bird's-foot-trefoil, clover, black medick and restharrow. In the south of England the common blue may be found with other blue butterflies, particularly chalk-hill, Adonis and silver-studded. Most of the blues are found on the North and South Downs where their food plants grow.

Only the male common blue has the showy metallic markings that make the wings glitter in the summer sun; the females are usually brown. The bright blue colour is produced by the diffraction of sunlight by thousands of corrugated scales on the wings which absorb all colours of the spectrum except blue. The wings contain no blue pigment.

Two generations are produced each year – sometimes three in the south of England – and each butterfly lives for about three weeks. Groups of males may be found clustering around puddles, drinking the water for its mineral content.

Notes and Sketches

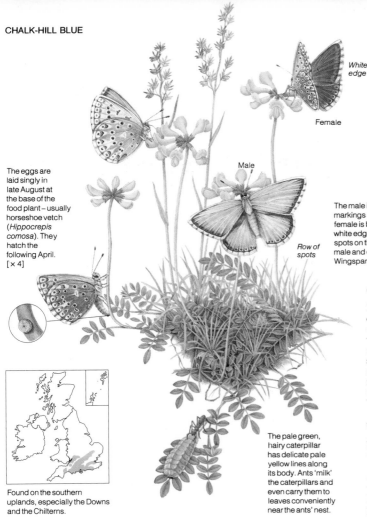

White edge

Female

Male

Row of spots

The eggs are laid singly in late August at the base of the food plant – usually horseshoe vetch (*Hippocrepis comosa*). They hatch the following April. [× 4]

The chrysalis forms in June or July on the ground beneath the food plant and hatches in about a month.

The male is silvery-blue with dark markings around the fore-wings; the female is brown. Both sexes have a white edge to the wings and a row of spots on the hind-wing – black in the male and orange in the female. Wingspan 1⅜ in. (35 mm).

The pale green, hairy caterpillar has delicate pale yellow lines along its body. Ants 'milk' the caterpillars and even carry them to leaves conveniently near the ants' nest.

Found on the southern uplands, especially the Downs and the Chilterns.

SITES GUIDE

There are many similarities between the chalk-hill blue and the Adonis blue. The food plant of both of their caterpillars is the relatively rare horseshoe vetch. Fortunately, their larvae hatch at different times. These butterflies can be seen on chalk hills in southern and south-western England.

Chalk-hill blue *Lysandra coridon*

Like many blues, the chalk-hill blue has males that are brightly coloured to attract females, and females that are drab to conceal them from predators. Both have spots on the underside of the wings but the spotting can be very variable. The males spend much time basking in the sun with wings open. They used to be seen in great numbers in their preferred localities – on chalky slopes, as their name suggests. The butterflies take nectar from many wild flowers and, like the Adonis blue, are also attracted to dung. There is only one generation a year, in July and August. The butterflies live up to 20 days.

The caterpillars are usually found on horseshoe vetch, but they also eat bird's-foot-trefoil and kidney vetch. Like the Adonis and silver-studded blues, the caterpillars are protected by ants, which keep away predators. The ants gain by 'milking' the caterpillars of a sweet fluid which they secrete.

The chalk-hill blue's decline – and even extinction in Lincolnshire, for example – has been attributed to myxomatosis, which seriously reduced the rabbit population. Where rabbits have ceased to graze, scrub has grown up and killed off the food plants. Ploughing of old pastures also destroys the food plants.

Notes and Sketches

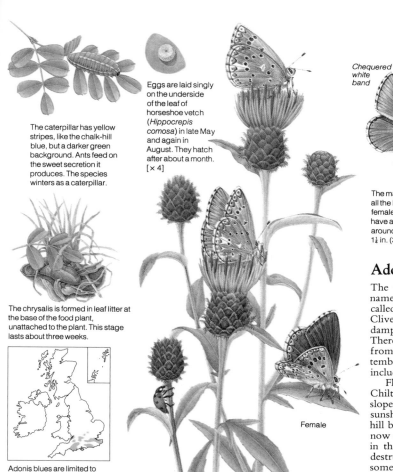

The caterpillar has yellow stripes, like the chalk-hill blue, but a darker green background. Ants feed on the sweet secretion it produces. The species winters as a caterpillar.

The chrysalis is formed in leaf litter at the base of the food plant, unattached to the plant. This stage lasts about three weeks.

Adonis blues are limited to chalk and limestone areas in the south of England.

Eggs are laid singly on the underside of the leaf of horseshoe vetch (*Hippocrepis comosa*) in late May and again in August. They hatch after about a month. [× 4]

Chequered white band

Male

The male is the brightest blue of all the British butterflies; the female is brown. Both sexes have a chequered white band around all the wings. Wingspan 1¼ in. (32 mm).

Female

SITES GUIDE

At first glance, the sight of a crowd of these beautiful butterflies feeding on dung is disconcerting as the two do not seem to be compatible. Nevertheless, it is not uncommon and the minerals so gained clearly provide a necessary supplement to the butterflies' diet. Adonis blues are rare and sites have not been included in this book.

Adonis blue *Lysandra bellargus*

The vivid blue of the males is so striking that the species is named after Adonis, the god of masculine beauty. It used to be called the Clifden Blue after one of its first known localities at Cliveden in Buckinghamshire. Males will congregate to drink at damp sand or dung, where they obtain salts essential to them. There are two generations a year and butterflies are on the wing from mid-May to mid-June and again in August and September. They feed on the nectar of a variety of wild flowers including vetches, trefoils, clovers and marjoram.

Flower-rich grassy slopes and hollows on the Downs and Chilterns are the places where Adonis blues might be seen. The slopes they prefer face south or west and receive plenty of sunshine. The Adonis blue may be seen flying with the chalk-hill blue but is much more local in its distribution. Indeed it is now declining rapidly in Britain and has recently become extinct in three-quarters of its former localities. The loss is due to destruction of its food plants, sometimes through ploughing, sometimes through the invasion of scrub which rabbits formerly kept down. It is likely to become extinct in Britain during the 1990s unless conservation measures are undertaken.

Notes and Sketches

The eggs are laid singly at the base of leaves of bird's-foot-trefoil. [× 4]

Female

The caterpillars eat the buds, flowers and pods of the food plant. They hibernate on the plant.

SITES GUIDE

In addition to its short 'tails' which are hard to distinguish, this butterfly has banded antennae and black and white margins to its wings which make it easier for the fortunate observer to identify it. Short-tailed blues have not been recorded at any of the sites in this book.

Male

The chrysalis is attached to a trefoil leaf by a silk girdle and pad.

Mazarine blue
Cyaniris semiargus

This former British resident became extinct early in the 1900s. Mazarine blues from Europe occasionally visit the south coast in summer. Wingspan 1¼ in. (32 mm).

Short 'tail'

A rare and irregular migrant that may be seen south of a line from London to Bristol.

The male has violet wings; the female has brown wings with faint blue colouring at the base. Both sexes have tiny 'tails' on the hind-wings. They are shown on bird's-foot-trefoil (*Lotus corniculatus*). Wingspan 1 in. (25 mm).

Short-tailed blue *Everes argiades*

This exceedingly rare migrant to England flies across the English Channel from northern France where it breeds successfully. It lays its eggs on bird's-foot-trefoil and medick and is most likely to be found on heathlands, rough pastures and flowery hillsides. The butterfly was first recorded in Britain in 1885, and was called Bloxworth blue after Bloxworth Heath in Dorset where it was captured. Shortly afterwards other specimens were discovered in old collections, including one in a collection made 25 years earlier; it had been captured at Blackpool.

The tiny 'tails' are not easy to see and are covered in large scales, appearing hairy. The upper side of the male is similar to the silver-studded blue or common blue and the underside to the holly blue. As a migrant from France, the butterfly is most likely to be found in southern England. It has never been recorded breeding here, but there is a chance that highly localised colonies might exist in Devon, Cornwall, Dorset and Avon where it has been recorded mostly in the past.

The mazarine blue is another very rare migrant to England which may sometimes be found around red clover, thrift, kidney vetch or melilot plants in summer.

Notes and Sketches

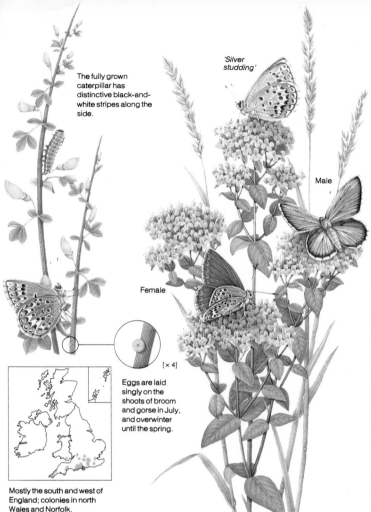

The fully grown caterpillar has distinctive black-and-white stripes along the side.

'Silver studding'

Male

Female

[× 4]

Eggs are laid singly on the shoots of broom and gorse in July, and overwinter until the spring.

Mostly the south and west of England; colonies in north Wales and Norfolk.

The pale chrysalis is formed at the base of the food plant on a loosely made silk net.

The male is silvery blue, with a white edge outside a black strip. The female is brown, with orange markings. The undersides are spotted with black, blue and orange – the blue spots giving the impression of 'silver studding'. Wingspan 1⅜ in. (35 mm).

SITES GUIDE

The loss of large numbers of rabbits as a result of myxomatosis has had far-reaching effects during the past thirty years or so, and has caused a decline in some populations of butterflies, such as the silver-studded blue. Keep a look out for this insect at the National Trust sites in southern England.

Silver-studded blue *Plebejus argus*

This attractive butterfly with its unique row of silver spots is typical of the diminishing heathland of Britain. Since the Second World War large areas of heath have been turned into farm land, removing food plants such as gorse, broom and heather. As a result, the butterfly has become extinct in Kent and probably in mid-Wales, central Norfolk and Dartmoor.

Where its food plants remain, as in parts of north Wales, the Ashdown Forest in Sussex, and the New Forest, the silver-studded blue can be common. The butterfly expert E. B. Ford wrote in 1945: 'The entomologist who in mid-July steps from his car in one of the great tracts of heather in the New Forest will find himself surrounded by immense numbers of this butterfly.' The numbers now, however, even in favourite spots, are probably smaller because of an indirect threat to the food plants – myxomatosis. The disease has reduced the rabbit population, allowing grass to grow and swamp the plants.

The caterpillars of the silver-studded blue are attractive to ants which milk them of a sweet secretion produced by their bodies. The ants even carry them to food plants in return for the free food supply.

Notes and Sketches

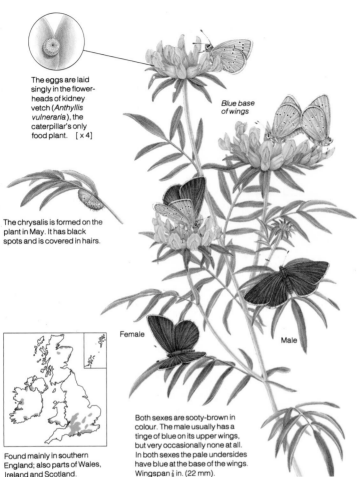

The eggs are laid singly in the flower-heads of kidney vetch (*Anthyllis vulneraria*), the caterpillar's only food plant. [x 4]

Blue base of wings

The chrysalis is formed on the plant in May. It has black spots and is covered in hairs.

The caterpillar feeds on the flowers of the kidney vetch. In July, when fully grown, it hibernates until the following spring.

Female

Male

Found mainly in southern England; also parts of Wales, Ireland and Scotland.

Both sexes are sooty-brown in colour. The male usually has a tinge of blue on its upper wings, but very occasionally none at all. In both sexes the pale undersides have blue at the base of the wings. Wingspan ⅞ in. (22 mm).

SITES GUIDE

The larvae of this butterfly may be yellow or buff in colour with dark heads and delicate markings along their backs and sides. They are rather squat in appearance and turn into hairy pupae. Small blues may sometimes be seen at National Trust sites in southern England and occasionally in parts of Wales, Ireland and Scotland.

Small blue *Cupido minimus*

These frail little butterflies – the smallest in Britain – are vigorous flyers as they flit from flower to flower drinking the nectar. They can be quite numerous in sheltered localities, skimming low to the vegetation and even flying through thickets where they are well camouflaged by their colouring. The constant movement through plants gradually wears the scales off their wings, and the butterflies lose their colour, develop ragged edges, and become rather pathetic flyers. By the end of their two-week life they flutter ineffectually to the ground where they are likely to be eaten by ants or birds.

The small blue is found mostly in southern and central England in chalk and limestone country where its food plant, kidney vetch, grows well. But it is not exclusively associated with chalk and limestone. It is also found in coastal areas of South Wales, Scotland and parts of Ireland. The butterfly lives on downland slopes and in hollows, inside old sheltered chalk quarries, along disused railway cuttings, on sandhills and on coastal cliffs. Recently it has declined in Yorkshire, but a new breeding area has been discovered on the Cumbrian coast. The butterfly is on the wing from late May to the end of June.

Notes and Sketches

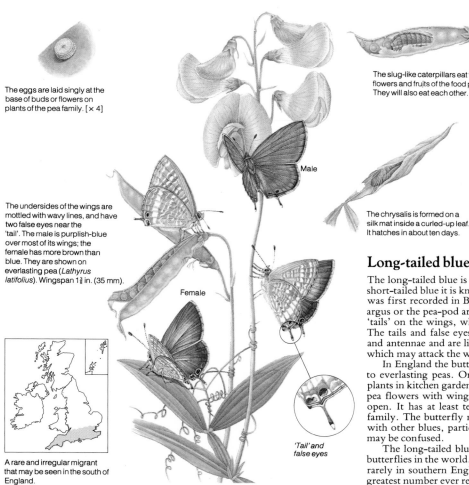

The eggs are laid singly at the base of buds or flowers on plants of the pea family. [× 4]

The undersides of the wings are mottled with wavy lines, and have two false eyes near the 'tail'. The male is purplish-blue over most of its wings; the female has more brown than blue. They are shown on everlasting pea (*Lathyrus latifolius*). Wingspan 1⅜ in. (35 mm).

Male

Female

A rare and irregular migrant that may be seen in the south of England.

'Tail' and false eyes

The slug-like caterpillars eat the flowers and fruits of the food plant. They will also eat each other.

The chrysalis is formed on a silk mat inside a curled-up leaf. It hatches in about ten days.

SITES GUIDE

The sheer scarcity of this butterfly coupled with the fact that it generally rests with its wings closed and with only its camouflaged undersides visible, means that the possibility of seeing a long-tailed blue in England is most unlikely. The keen entomologist would do better to travel to tropical or sub-tropical Africa in search of this insect.

Long-tailed blue *Lampides boeticus*

The long-tailed blue is a rare migrant to Britain, but unlike the short-tailed blue it is known to breed here. The long-tailed blue was first recorded in Brighton in 1859 and called the Brighton argus or the pea-pod argus. Its present name describes the two 'tails' on the wings, which often become twisted and broken. The tails and false eyes mimic the butterfly's compound eyes and antennae and are likely to confuse predators such as birds, which may attack the wrong end of the body.

In England the butterfly has been recorded in gardens close to everlasting peas. On the Continent it can be a pest on pea plants in kitchen gardens and is often seen drinking nectar from pea flowers with wings shut or basking in the sun with wings open. It has at least ten food plants, all members of the pea family. The butterfly may also be found in flowery meadows with other blues, particularly the common blue with which it may be confused.

The long-tailed blue is one of the most widely distributed butterflies in the world. However it is likely to be seen only very rarely in southern England, between July and September. The greatest number ever recorded in Britain was 31 in 1945.

Notes and Sketches

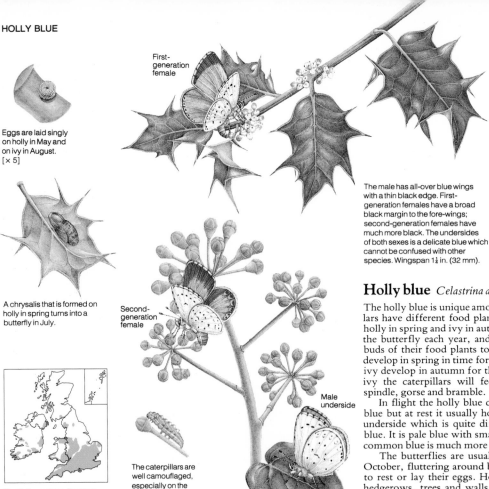

Eggs are laid singly on holly in May and on ivy in August. [× 5]

A chrysalis that is formed on holly in spring turns into a butterfly in July.

Mostly in southern England; also parts of Wales, Ireland and Scotland.

First-generation female

Second-generation female

The caterpillars are well camouflaged, especially on the buds of ivy.

The male has all-over blue wings with a thin black edge. First-generation females have a broad black margin to the fore-wings; second-generation females have much more black. The undersides of both sexes is a delicate blue which cannot be confused with other species. Wingspan 1¼ in. (32 mm).

Male underside

SITES GUIDE

The holly blue is often seen in gardens because that is where the food plants of its larvae, especially holly, are frequently cultivated. The adults rarely feed on flowers but will drink at puddles and enjoy sweet sap where trees have been damaged. Holly blues may be seen at most sites in southern England and parts of Wales and Ireland.

Holly blue *Celastrina argiolus*

The holly blue is unique among British butterflies as its caterpillars have different food plants at different times of the year – holly in spring and ivy in autumn. There are two generations of the butterfly each year, and the caterpillars prefer the flower buds of their food plants to the leaves. The buds of the holly develop in spring in time for one generation, and the buds of the ivy develop in autumn for the other. In the absence of holly or ivy the caterpillars will feed on the flowers of dogwood, spindle, gorse and bramble.

In flight the holly blue can be confused with the common blue but at rest it usually holds its wings closed, showing the underside which is quite different from that of the common blue. It is pale blue with small black spots; the underside of the common blue is much more colourful.

The butterflies are usually seen, from late March to mid-October, fluttering around bushes and trees looking for places to rest or lay their eggs. Holly trees in spring and ivy-bound hedgerows, trees and walls in summer particularly attract it. The holly blue is typically a hedgerow butterfly but it is also found on scrubby hillsides and in woodland clearings.

Notes and Sketches

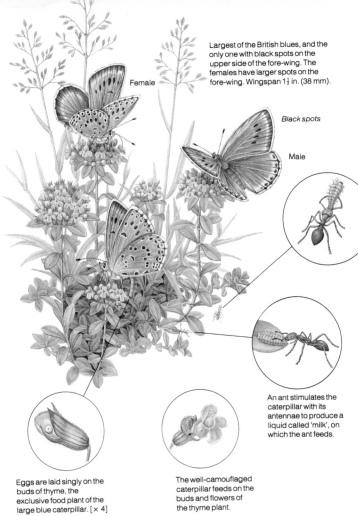

Female

Largest of the British blues, and the only one with black spots on the upper side of the fore-wing. The females have larger spots on the fore-wing. Wingspan 1½ in. (38 mm).

Black spots

Male

A pale chrysalis, unprotected by any cocoon, is formed in the ants' nest. The butterfly hatches three weeks later.

The caterpillar is carried off to the ants' nest where it feeds on ant grubs in return for providing more 'milk'. It hibernates in the nest through winter.

An ant stimulates the caterpillar with its antennae to produce a liquid called 'milk', on which the ant feeds.

Eggs are laid singly on the buds of thyme, the exclusive food plant of the large blue caterpillar. [× 4]

The well-camouflaged caterpillar feeds on the buds and flowers of the thyme plant.

SITES GUIDE

The extinction of this butterfly in the British Isles in 1979 is an example of the effect on wildlife of rapid changes to its habitat. Unless they are very adaptable, most species simply die out. Often, too little is known about their lifestyle and habits to be able to monitor the significance of such changes before it is too late.

Large blue *Maculinea arion*

The large blue was discovered in 1795 and became extinct in Britain 184 years later in 1979. However, the butterfly now flies again following the successful release of Swedish forms at a secret West Country site. The extinction of the large blue followed changes in agricultural practice that disrupted its complex life-cycle. The butterfly had evolved an intimate association with wild thyme and with a species of ant, *Myrmica sabuleti*. The female butterflies laid their eggs on thyme plants, and after the caterpillars hatched they were carried off by the ants. In the ants' nest the caterpillars ate ant grubs in return for allowing the ants to 'milk' them of a sweet bodily secretion.

Large blues died out in areas where grazing land was ploughed up, destroying the thyme. But they also died out in areas where no ploughing was done. During the 1970s it was discovered that the butterflies thrived only where grass was grazed short by cattle, sheep or rabbits. Where farm grazing had been reduced, or rabbits had been eliminated by myxomatosis, the grass grew long and the butterflies were unable to find the thyme. The drought of 1976 reduced the last colony to 16 butterflies, and in 1979 no eggs were produced at all.

Notes and Sketches

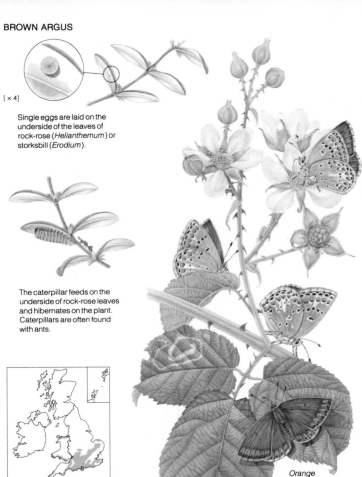

[× 4]

Single eggs are laid on the underside of the leaves of rock-rose (*Helianthemum*) or storksbill (*Erodium*).

The caterpillar feeds on the underside of rock-rose leaves and hibernates on the plant. Caterpillars are often found with ants.

Found in the south of England and the north and south coasts of Wales.

The chrysalis is formed at the base of the plant, among plant debris.

Dark brown with orange half-moons around the edge of the wings. Both sexes have a black spot in the centre of the fore-wings. The female is slightly larger and lighter coloured than the male. Wingspan 1⅛ in. (28 mm).

Orange half-moons

SITES GUIDE

Despite its colour, this argus is considered one of the blues. It is fairly easy to differentiate between the sexes of the other members of this family by coloration alone – the males are bluer than the females. The two sexes in the brown and northern brown are very alike. It may be seen at 9, 10, 12, 14–17, 19, 21, 27.

Brown argus *Aricia agestis*

The brown argus is a gregarious butterfly, usually seen in the sunshine with a group of others flitting among bramble flowers, bird's-foot-trefoil or the other wild flowers on which it feeds. At dusk, or on dull days, groups can be found roosting together head down on long grass stems, often in the company of common blues. There are two generations each year, with butterflies on the wing in May and June and again in July and August. Each butterfly lives for about three weeks. Courting males are said to smell strongly of chocolate. The caterpillars are often found with ants, which 'milk' them of secretions. The ants may be beneficial to the caterpillars in deterring predators.

The brown argus is not a typical 'blue' because it lacks the bright blue colours. It is easily confused with females of the common, chalk-hill, Adonis, and silver-studded blues. The species was first described in 1717 and was then thought to include the northern brown argus. The dividing line between the two seems to run through South Yorkshire. Distribution of the brown argus repeats the pattern of the chalk and limestone areas in south and central England. It can also be found on sandy coastal slopes where common storksbill grows.

Notes and Sketches

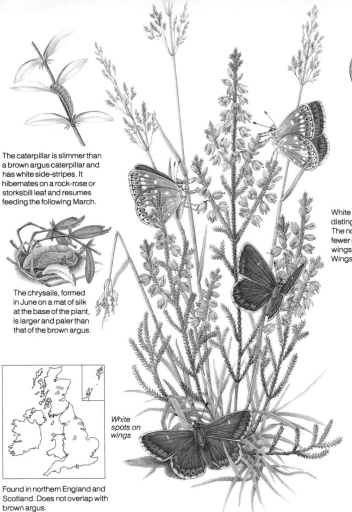

The caterpillar is slimmer than a brown argus caterpillar and has white side-stripes. It hibernates on a rock-rose or storksbill leaf and resumes feeding the following March.

The chrysalis, formed in June on a mat of silk at the base of the plant, is larger and paler than that of the brown argus.

Found in northern England and Scotland. Does not overlap with brown argus.

White spots on wings

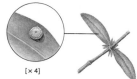

[× 4]

Single eggs are laid on the upper surface of the leaves of various rock-rose and storksbill species. They hatch after about two weeks.

White spots on the fore-wings distinguish it from the brown argus. The northern brown argus also has fewer orange half-moons on the fore-wings. Shown on heather. Wingspan 1⅛ in. (28 mm).

Sites Guide

The caterpillars of the whole of the blue family differ from those of other butterflies by being shaped like a woodlouse. Those of the brown argus hatch in August and manage to survive hibernation. This butterfly has been recorded in and around a few of the sites in this book but its rarity prevents their identification.

Northern brown argus *Aricia artaxerxes*

Entomologists from any part of Britain who wanted to see this butterfly in the 18th century had to journey to Edinburgh and scramble on the steep, tussocky slopes of Arthur's Seat, an ancient volcano near the city centre. That was the only locality where *artaxerxes* was then known to live. It was then thought to be a form of the brown argus when that species was first described in 1717. Later it was classified as a species, then as a variation of the brown argus, and later still as a sub-species. Finally, in 1967, it was again given separate species status.

The two species are similar in their food plants and in behaviour, but the northern brown argus is not gregarious. Each male claims a territory as its own and drives away other males. There is only one generation a year. The adults are on the wing from mid-June into August.

Names for the butterfly have been as diverse as its classification. Scotch white spot aptly describes its distinguishing feature. Other names are mountain and Scotch argus, which can cause confusion with the other more commonly called Scotch argus. A sub-species, *salmacis*, found in the southern part of the range, was called Durham or Castle Eden argus.

Notes and Sketches

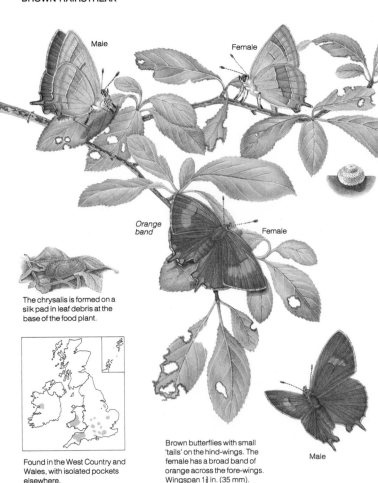

Male

Female

The caterpillar hatches in spring and begins feeding on the young sloe leaves. It lives for about 75 days and is fully grown by the end of June.

Eggs are laid singly on the twigs of sloe (*Prunus spinosa*), and remain dormant through the winter – for seven or eight months. [× 8]

Orange band

Female

The chrysalis is formed on a silk pad in leaf debris at the base of the food plant.

Found in the West Country and Wales, with isolated pockets elsewhere.

Brown butterflies with small 'tails' on the hind-wings. The female has a broad band of orange across the fore-wings. Wingspan 1⅜ in. (35 mm).

Male

SITES GUIDE

The brown hairstreak is unlike many other species of butterfly, such as the common blue and the orange tip, in that the female is more brightly coloured than the male. It also flies high in the tree tops where it is almost impossible for entomologists to see it. The brown hairstreak is rare and has been noted only at a few Irish sites in this book.

Brown hairstreak *Thecla betulae*

In the 18th century butterflies whose sexes looked different were often thought to be two separate species. The colourful female of this butterfly was then called the golden hairstreak.

The brown hairstreak is an autumn species and flies between August and October, each butterfly living about three weeks. It is intimately associated with woodlands and hedgerows. The butterflies congregate around trees in woodland glades to conduct their courtship. They feed on the prolific honeydew exuded on leaves by aphids. And they perch high in the trees with their relatives the purple hairstreaks. Thickets of bramble and sloe – so typical of English woods and old hedgerows – attract the egg-laying females, which drink the nectar of the bramble flowers and lay their eggs on the leaves of sloe. By the time the chrysalis stage is reached, however, 90 per cent of the caterpillars and chrysalises have been eaten by predators – the caterpillars by birds, the chrysalises by small mammals.

The brown hairstreak has now become extinct in East Anglia and the south-east of England. The process has probably been hastened by hedge-cutting which can kill about half the eggs laid on the young growth of sloe each year.

Notes and Sketches

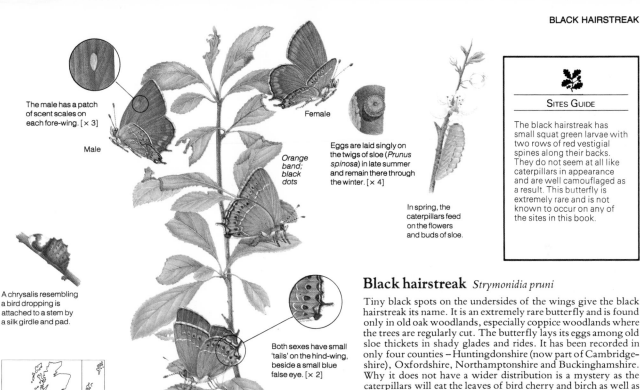

The male has a patch of scent scales on each fore-wing. [× 3]

Male

Female

Orange band; black dots

Eggs are laid singly on the twigs of sloe (*Prunus spinosa*) in late summer and remain there through the winter. [× 4]

In spring, the caterpillars feed on the flowers and buds of sloe.

A chrysalis resembling a bird dropping is attached to a stem by a silk girdle and pad.

Both sexes have small 'tails' on the hind-wing, beside a small blue false eye. [× 2]

Found only in traditional coppice woodland of the east Midlands.

Despite the name, the butterflies are brown rather than black, and have orange markings. The female has more orange on the fore-wings than the male. The underside has a prominent orange band with black spots. Wingspan 1¼ in. (32 mm).

SITES GUIDE

The black hairstreak has small squat green larvae with two rows of red vestigial spines along their backs. They do not seem at all like caterpillars in appearance and are well camouflaged as a result. This butterfly is extremely rare and is not known to occur on any of the sites in this book.

Black hairstreak *Strymonidia pruni*

Tiny black spots on the undersides of the wings give the black hairstreak its name. It is an extremely rare butterfly and is found only in old oak woodlands, especially coppice woodlands where the trees are regularly cut. The butterfly lays its eggs among old sloe thickets in shady glades and rides. It has been recorded in only four counties – Huntingdonshire (now part of Cambridgeshire), Oxfordshire, Northamptonshire and Buckinghamshire. Why it does not have a wider distribution is a mystery as the caterpillars will eat the leaves of bird cherry and birch as well as the leaves of sloe. The single generation of black hairstreaks are on the wing in June and July.

Half of the known colonies of the black hairstreak have become extinct in the last few decades. There are now fewer than 30 colonies left in England, and extinction from the British Isles is a real possibility. Some colonies have disappeared because of loss of deciduous woodlands and the creation of arable farmland. The butterflies spend a lot of time resting high up on the leaves of oak trees where they drink the sugary honey–dew left on the leaves by aphids. They also visit privet, wayfaring trees and brambles to take nectar from the flowers.

Notes and Sketches

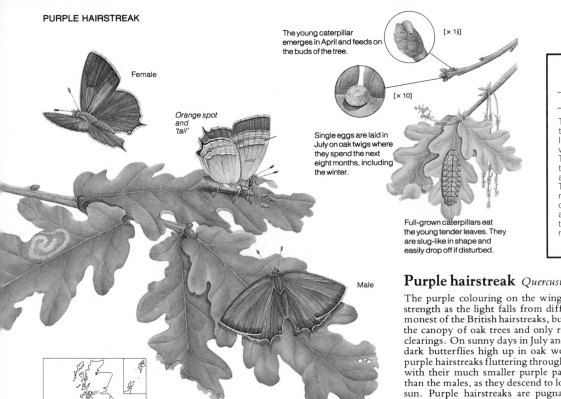

Female

Orange spot and 'tail'

The young caterpillar emerges in April and feeds on the buds of the tree.

[× 1½]

Single eggs are laid in July on oak twigs where they spend the next eight months, including the winter.

[× 10]

Full-grown caterpillars eat the young tender leaves. They are slug-like in shape and easily drop off if disturbed.

Male

The males have a purple iridescence over all the wings. The females have a V-like area of purple on the fore-wings only. The undersides of both sexes are identical, with a white 'hairstreak', an orange spot and a tiny 'tail'. Wingspan 1⅜ in. (34 mm).

Mostly in southern England and Wales. Now extremely local in Ireland.

The chrysalis is formed on the tree or at the base, at the end of May or in June.

SITES GUIDE

The name 'hairstreak' refers to the fine white and black line on the undersides of the wings of these butterflies. This line is said to resemble the mark left in damp paint if a hair is drawn across it. These butterflies have been recorded in and around a few of the sites in this book although precise reference to these is prevented by their rarity.

Purple hairstreak *Quercusia quercus*

The purple colouring on the wings of this butterfly varies in strength as the light falls from different angles. It is the commonest of the British hairstreaks, but is seldom seen, as it lives in the canopy of oak trees and only rarely descends to paths and clearings. On sunny days in July and August, the movement of dark butterflies high up in oak woods may reveal groups of purple hairstreaks fluttering through the branches. The females, with their much smaller purple patches, are seen more often than the males, as they descend to lower branches to bask in the sun. Purple hairstreaks are pugnacious butterflies, and will attack other insects which stray into their territory, and even have squabbles with wasps. They feed on the sugar-rich honey-dew deposited by aphids on ash and aspen leaves. Flowers are rarely visited for nectar, but the butterflies are occasionally seen feeding from the flowers of sweet chestnut and brambles.

The purple hairstreak is a true woodland butterfly, and its close association with oak trees is reflected in its scientific name which twice uses the Latin word *quercus*, meaning 'oak'. The caterpillars have been found on sweet chestnut and sallow, as well as oak, but they are probably only secondary food plants.

Notes and Sketches

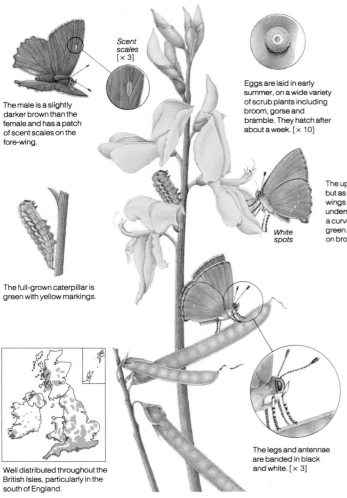

Scent scales [× 3]

The male is a slightly darker brown than the female and has a patch of scent scales on the fore-wing.

The full-grown caterpillar is green with yellow markings.

Well distributed throughout the British Isles, particularly in the south of England.

Eggs are laid in early summer, on a wide variety of scrub plants including broom, gorse and bramble. They hatch after about a week. [× 10]

White spots

The upper surface of the wings is brown, but as the butterfly always rests with its wings closed the vivid green of the undersides is often seen. The 'hairstreak' is a curved line of white spots against the green. These butterflies are shown resting on broom. Wingspan 1⅛ in. (28 mm).

The chrysalis is formed in debris at the base of the plant, and there spends winter. It makes a creaking or scratching sound, presumably to deter predators.

The legs and antennae are banded in black and white. [× 3]

Sites Guide

The caterpillar of this butterfly feeds on a range of common shrubs including gorse, broom, bramble and buckthorn which occur throughout the British Isles and Ireland. The larva actually feeds on the developing fruits rather than the leaves of these plants. Green hairstreaks may be seen at 1, 9, 13, 15, 24, 25, 27, 28, 40, 41, 45, 47, 53–57, 61–63.

Green hairstreak *Callophrys rubi*

The green metallic colour of the underside is unique among British butterflies. It is produced by the effects of light on the microscopic scales which cover the wings, resulting in only the green colour of the spectrum reaching the viewer's eye. The green hairstreak is unusual in other ways, too. Hairstreak butterflies get their name from the hair-like line across the underside of the wings, but on the green hairstreak this is reduced to a row of white dots. The species is the only British hairstreak which does not have small 'tails' on the hind-wings. And it hibernates as a chrysalis, while all other hairstreaks spend the winter as eggs.

The green hairstreak is a familiar butterfly in spring and early summer. It is also Britain's most common hairstreak as its caterpillars have at least ten food plants. Its favourite haunts include scrubby areas on downland, heathland and wasteland, together with woodland clearings and tracks. The butterflies are hardly ever seen feeding on the nectar of flowers. Instead they congregate in secluded corners, establishing territories, perching on vantage points and chasing each other in short bursts of swift flight around scrub bushes.

Notes and Sketches

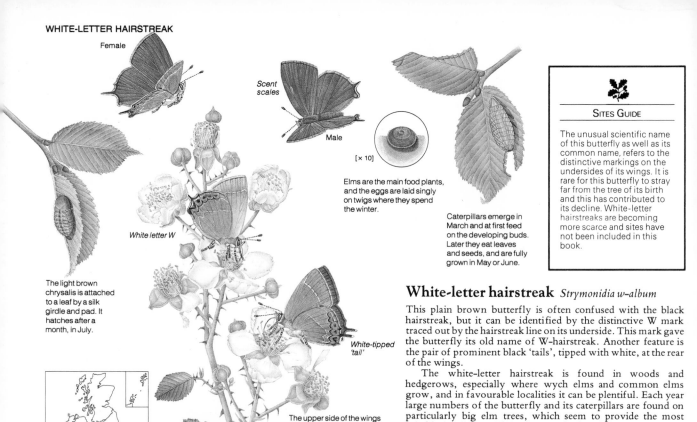

Female

Scent scales

Male

[× 10]

White letter W

White-tipped 'tail'

Elms are the main food plants, and the eggs are laid singly on twigs where they spend the winter.

Caterpillars emerge in March and at first feed on the developing buds. Later they eat leaves and seeds, and are fully grown in May or June.

The light brown chrysalis is attached to a leaf by a silk girdle and pad. It hatches after a month, in July.

Wide distribution in England and Wales, as far as north Yorkshire.

The upper side of the wings is dark brown. The female has a slightly longer 'tail', and the male has patches of scent scales on the forewings. The lighter underside has a white letter W close to the tail. The butterflies are shown feeding on bramble flowers. Wingspan 1¼ in. (32 mm).

SITES GUIDE

The unusual scientific name of this butterfly as well as its common name, refers to the distinctive markings on the undersides of its wings. It is rare for this butterfly to stray far from the tree of its birth and this has contributed to its decline. White-letter hairstreaks are becoming more scarce and sites have not been included in this book.

White-letter hairstreak *Strymonidia w-album*

This plain brown butterfly is often confused with the black hairstreak, but it can be identified by the distinctive W mark traced out by the hairstreak line on its underside. This mark gave the butterfly its old name of W-hairstreak. Another feature is the pair of prominent black 'tails', tipped with white, at the rear of the wings.

The white-letter hairstreak is found in woods and hedgerows, especially where wych elms and common elms grow, and in favourable localities it can be plentiful. Each year large numbers of the butterfly and its caterpillars are found on particularly big elm trees, which seem to provide the most suitable conditions. They also spend a lot of their time visiting bramble and privet blossom for the nectar and the honeydew deposited on the leaves by aphids. They walk over leaves, opening and closing their wings, like their relatives the green hairstreaks and small coppers. White-letter hairstreaks are on the wing in July and August, and each butterfly lives for about 20 days. The loss of elms from Dutch elm disease in the 1970s removed many food plants, but the butterfly may be exploiting growths of scrub elm – suckers that grow up around dead trees.

Notes and Sketches

The chrysalis is attached to a stem or leaf by a silk girdle and pad. It hatches after three or four weeks.

[× 2]
Small coppers will occasionally be seen with a row of blue spots across the hind-wings.

The eggs are laid on the upper surface of the leaves of sorrel and dock (*Rumex* species), and occasionally knotgrass (*Polygonum*). They hatch after a week. [× 10]

SITES GUIDE

This bright little butterfly is one of the last to be seen on the wing in the autumn. It is an adaptable insect whose common food plants are not confined to specialised habitats but grow readily in a wide variety of situations enabling the small copper to live throughout most of the British Isles. It can be seen at most of the sites in this book.

The hairy caterpillar is well camouflaged for its life on sorrel leaves. There are two colour forms – green and green-pink. There may be three generations a year and the caterpillars of the last generation hibernate.

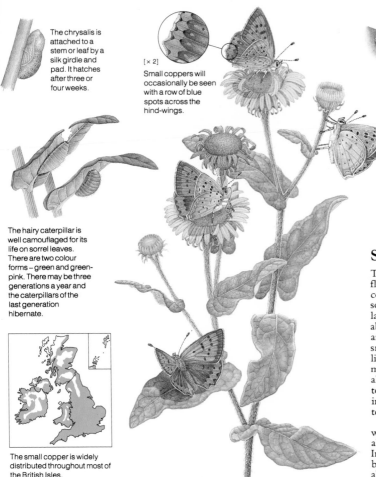

The wings are copper-coloured with black markings on the fore-wings. These butterflies are shown on fleabane (*Pulicaria dysenterica*), a favourite nectar source. Wingspan 1⅛ in. (28 mm).

The small copper is widely distributed throughout most of the British Isles.

Small copper *Lycaena phlaeas*

The Yorkshire lepidopterist Adrian Haworth called this butterfly the common copper in 1803. True to its old name, it is still common in suitable places between April and October. It is the sole remaining member of the British coppers, as its relative the large copper became extinct in the fenland in 1865. The key to its abundance is that the caterpillar eats a variety of common dock and sorrel species which are widely distributed in Britain. The small copper frequents urban gardens and the verges of railway lines, roads and motorways, as well as heaths, downland and meadows. It is often in the company of blue butterflies, and is always found near flowers. It is a bright butterfly which is easy to spot as it basks, with wings open, on flowers or darts off to intercept rival blues, small heaths and hairstreaks that fly into its territory.

Variations in the size of the spots on the fore-wings and the width of the copper band on the hind-wing occur often, and albino specimens are known. There is a distinct sub-species in Ireland in which the band on the underside of the hind-wing is broader than on small coppers in Britain. Each butterfly lives for about a month.

Notes and Sketches

MEADOW BROWN

The eggs are laid singly in summer on several types of grass including cocksfoot and *Poa* species. [× 2]

The caterpillars have a prolonged development period of eight to nine months. They feed at night during mild spells throughout winter.

A pale green chrysalis with black stripes is formed at the base of the food plant in May or June.

The male is smaller than the female, and much darker, with less prominent false eyes.

The female has a single prominent false eye on each fore-wing. It stands out strongly against the large orange patch.

The false eyes sometimes have a subsidiary pupil as well as the major one.

The butterflies rest for the night, head up, on grass stems. All the browns, like the aristocrats and the fritillaries, have only four functional legs.

Notes and Sketches

Two white pupils

Male

Female

The eggs are laid singly at the base of a leaf of grass. Several species of grass are suitable, including meadow grass (*Poa annua*) and couch grass (*Agropyron repens*). [× 3]

Most common in southern England and Wales, and the south of Ireland.

Orange-brown butterflies that are usually found along hedgerows in July and August. The males are smaller and richer orange in colour than the females, with a distinct dark band of scent scales across the fore-wing. The false eye on the fore-wing of both sexes often has two white pupils. Wingspan of female 1½ in. (38 mm).

SITES GUIDE

The gatekeeper is so called because of its habit of staking out and defending territories around field corners, where gates and stiles are often located, especially if brambles, one of its favourite flowers, grow there. Gatekeepers are most common in the south of England and may be seen at most of the sites in this book.

Gatekeeper *Pyronia tithonus*

On sunny days in high summer, orange-brown butterflies flutter and settle along hedgerows and woodland paths. They are likely to be gatekeepers – also known as hedge browns because they are so often seen near country hedgerows. But the gatekeeper is easily mistaken for three other types of brown butterfly – the meadow brown, the speckled wood and the wall, which are also on the wing in July and August. They all have false eyes on their wings and are often found in the corners of fields near bramble thickets. However the wall is more likely to be seen basking on bare ground, while the gatekeeper visits hedgerows and the speckled wood enters woodland glades.

Male gatekeepers set up territories along hedgerows, and patrol them to keep out other insects. In search of sources of nectar, they are attracted to the flowers of marjoram, mint, wood sage and valerian, as well as bramble. And they are sometimes abundant in orchards. Each butterfly lives for about three weeks.

The caterpillars of the gatekeeper live from August until the following June, hibernating through the winter months low down among the grass.

Notes and Sketches

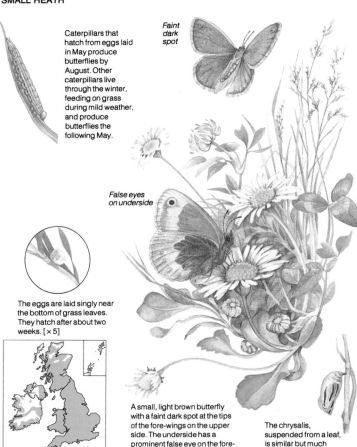

Caterpillars that hatch from eggs laid in May produce butterflies by August. Other caterpillars live through the winter, feeding on grass during mild weather, and produce butterflies the following May.

Faint dark spot

False eyes on underside

The eggs are laid singly near the bottom of grass leaves. They hatch after about two weeks. [× 5]

The small heath is found throughout Britain, with patchy distribution in Ireland.

A small, light brown butterfly with a faint dark spot at the tips of the fore-wings on the upper side. The underside has a prominent false eye on the fore-wing; the hind-wing is darker near the base and has a row of faint circles. Wingspan 1⅛ in. (28 mm).

The chrysalis, suspended from a leaf, is similar but much smaller than the chrysalis of the meadow brown. It hatches after a month.

Small heaths always close their wings when they are resting. The females are larger than the males.

SITES GUIDE

Fortunately, this butterfly can find the food plants for its larvae in many different locations. If it had been more confined to hay fields, then the current trend in agriculture towards early cuts of silage would have reduced its population. Small heaths are frequently seen and occur at most of the sites in this book except in Ireland.

Small heath *Coenonympha pamphilus*

This small tawny butterfly is very common throughout Britain during the summer wherever long grass grows. It is highly successful in this country because its caterpillars eat grass in both the uplands and the lowlands. Despite its name the small heath is not restricted to heathlands but can be numerous in areas ranging from urban wasteland to moorland, from meadows to railway embankments. It can be very common along roadside verges and ditches in September, often in the company of small coppers and common blues.

The butterflies live for about a month and are more often seen resting on grass than feeding from flowers. The warmer weather in the south of England allows for two generations a year. Butterflies may emerge from the chrysalis at any time between May and September since the caterpillar stage can develop as quickly as a month or as slowly as 11 months, including hibernation through the winter.

Despite the similarity between female and male, early butterfly enthusiasts had separate names for each sex – the selvedged heath brown for the male and the golden heath eye for the female.

Notes and Sketches

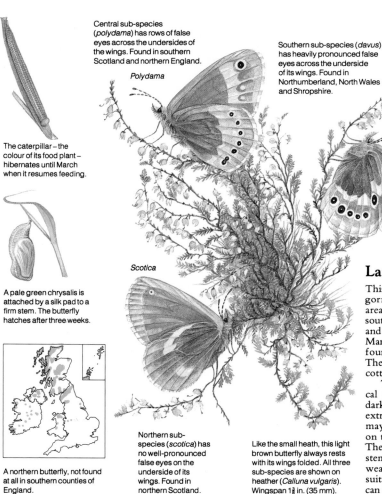

Central sub-species (*polydama*) has rows of false eyes across the undersides of the wings. Found in southern Scotland and northern England.

Polydama

Southern sub-species (*davus*) has heavily pronounced false eyes across the underside of its wings. Found in Northumberland, North Wales and Shropshire.

The caterpillar – the colour of its food plant – hibernates until March when it resumes feeding.

A pale green chrysalis is attached by a silk pad to a firm stem. The butterfly hatches after three weeks.

Eggs are laid singly on the leaves of white beak-sedge (*Rhynchospora alba*), the main food plant. They hatch after about two weeks. [× 7]

Davus

SITES GUIDE

The large heath is the only mountain butterfly to be found in Wales and Ireland. Its caterpillar hibernates and emerges in March to take advantage of new plant growth following the melting of the snows. Large heaths have been recorded at a few National Trust properties, but their rarity prevents the identification of these sites.

Scotica

A northern butterfly, not found at all in southern counties of England.

Northern sub-species (*scotica*) has no well-pronounced false eyes on the underside of its wings. Found in northern Scotland.

Like the small heath, this light brown butterfly always rests with its wings folded. All three sub-species are shown on heather (*Calluna vulgaris*). Wingspan 1⅜ in. (35 mm).

Large heath *Coenonympha tullia*

This is a butterfly of the British uplands, typical of the Cairngorms, the Cheviots and Snowdonia. In Ireland it flies in boggy areas and is at its southernmost point in the British Isles in south–west Ireland. It used to occur as far south as Lincolnshire and Staffordshire, and was called the Manchester Argus or Manchester Ringlet when discovered in 1795. The large heath is found on marshes, bogs and moors up to 2,000 ft (610 m). These wet areas support rich growths of sedges, fescues and cottongrass – all food plants for the caterpillars.

The large heath is unusual in having three distinct geographical sub-species which vary in colour and pattern, becoming darker to the south. There is one generation a year, but in the extreme north of Scotland and in the Orkneys the caterpillars may take two years to develop in the grass. The butterflies are on the wing in June and July and live for two or three weeks. They rarely visit flowers and are frequently seen resting on grass stems or turf. They fly very close to the ground in windy weather and rest low down in the grass on wet, dull days. In suitable areas the butterflies may be very numerous, and they can be seen 'dancing' about in the long grass of summer.

Notes and Sketches

RINGLET

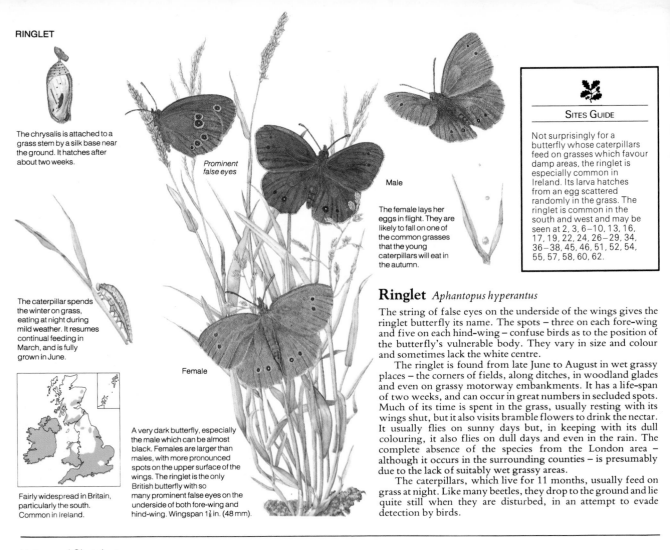

The chrysalis is attached to a grass stem by a silk base near the ground. It hatches after about two weeks.

The caterpillar spends the winter on grass, eating at night during mild weather. It resumes continual feeding in March, and is fully grown in June.

Fairly widespread in Britain, particularly the south. Common in Ireland.

Prominent false eyes

Male

The female lays her eggs in flight. They are likely to fall on one of the common grasses that the young caterpillars will eat in the autumn.

Female

A very dark butterfly, especially the male which can be almost black. Females are larger than males, with more pronounced spots on the upper surface of the wings. The ringlet is the only British butterfly with so many prominent false eyes on the underside of both fore-wing and hind-wing. Wingspan 1⅞ in. (48 mm).

SITES GUIDE

Not surprisingly for a butterfly whose caterpillars feed on grasses which favour damp areas, the ringlet is especially common in Ireland. Its larva hatches from an egg scattered randomly in the grass. The ringlet is common in the south and west and may be seen at 2, 3, 6–10, 13, 16, 17, 19, 22, 24, 26–29, 34, 36–38, 45, 46, 51, 52, 54, 55, 57, 58, 60, 62.

Ringlet *Aphantopus hyperantus*

The string of false eyes on the underside of the wings gives the ringlet butterfly its name. The spots – three on each fore-wing and five on each hind-wing – confuse birds as to the position of the butterfly's vulnerable body. They vary in size and colour and sometimes lack the white centre.

The ringlet is found from late June to August in wet grassy places – the corners of fields, along ditches, in woodland glades and even on grassy motorway embankments. It has a life-span of two weeks, and can occur in great numbers in secluded spots. Much of its time is spent in the grass, usually resting with its wings shut, but it also visits bramble flowers to drink the nectar. It usually flies on sunny days but, in keeping with its dull colouring, it also flies on dull days and even in the rain. The complete absence of the species from the London area – although it occurs in the surrounding counties – is presumably due to the lack of suitably wet grassy areas.

The caterpillars, which live for 11 months, usually feed on grass at night. Like many beetles, they drop to the ground and lie quite still when they are disturbed, in an attempt to evade detection by birds.

Notes and Sketches

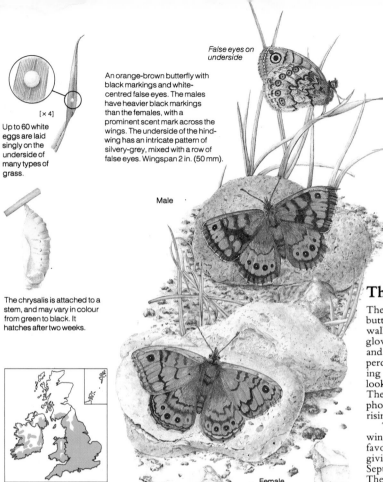

[× 4]

Up to 60 white eggs are laid singly on the underside of many types of grass.

An orange-brown butterfly with black markings and white-centred false eyes. The males have heavier black markings than the females, with a prominent scent mark across the wings. The underside of the hind-wing has an intricate pattern of silvery-grey, mixed with a row of false eyes. Wingspan 2 in. (50 mm).

False eyes on underside

Male

The chrysalis is attached to a stem, and may vary in colour from green to black. It hatches after two weeks.

Early summer caterpillars develop in a month. Late summer caterpillars hibernate, eating intermittently, until April.

Common in England and Wales; also found in southern Scotland and Ireland.

Female

SITES GUIDE

A butterfly as easily disturbed as the wall is a challenge to the wildlife photographer. One way of achieving success is to concentrate on a single individual, approaching it slowly and cautiously, until it eventually accepts your presence. Look for walls at 3, 5, 7, 9–14, 16, 17, 19–22, 24, 27–32, 36, 41, 45, 48, 52–54, 57, 59, 60.

The wall *Lasiommata megera*

The wall, or wall brown, is an energetic and brightly coloured butterfly which basks in the sunshine, often on warm rocks or walls, hence its name. Its rich orange colour may be seen glowing in the setting sun, as this is a butterfly that rises early and retires late. Males have strong territorial behaviour, and will perch on prominent places, making sorties to drive away intruding insects. They also patrol paths, hedgerows and fences looking for females, and visit wayside flowers to drink nectar. The wall is a restless butterfly and is easily disturbed when being photographed. It will accompany walkers in the countryside, rising up, flying further on and resting on the bare earth.

There are two broods of butterflies each year – the first on the wing in May and June, and the second in July and August. In very favourable seasons the first brood can appear as early as late April, giving rise to a second brood in June and July, and a third in September. The life-span of each butterfly is about three weeks. The wall could be confused with the speckled wood which might share the same lane. However the speckled wood prefers shady areas, while the wall is found in the open, obtaining as much sunshine as it can find.

Notes and Sketches

The eggs are laid singly on the leaves of purple moor grass (*Molinia caerulea*). [× 2]

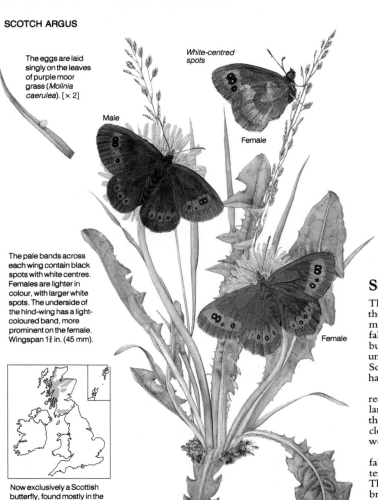

White-centred spots

Male

Female

The pale bands across each wing contain black spots with white centres. Females are lighter in colour, with larger white spots. The underside of the hind-wing has a light-coloured band, more prominent on the female. Wingspan 1⅜ in. (45 mm).

Female

Now exclusively a Scottish butterfly, found mostly in the west of the country.

The brown caterpillar feeds by night and rests on the base of the plant by day. It hibernates from September until April.

The chrysalis is formed in leaf litter at the base of the food plant, and hatches after about 16 days. [× 2]

SITES GUIDE

Although the Scotch argus is virtually confined to Scotland in the British Isles, it is a butterfly which is quite widespread in the rest of Europe. You might also expect it to survive further south because it obviously enjoys sunny weather. The Scotch argus may be seen at site 47.

Scotch argus *Erebia aethiops*

The rows of false eyes on the wings of this Scottish butterfly are the source of its name – from the hundred-eyed hero of Greek mythology who was constantly on the alert for enemies. The false eyes on the female are particularly well pronounced. As the butterflies shelter in the grass in rainy weather, the eyes on the underside peep out from above the hind-wings. At rest, the Scotch argus looks remarkably like a withered leaf, and males have been seen making approaches to dead leaves in the grass.

The butterfly delights in sunshine, especially in places which receive the warming rays of early morning. Edges of woodlands, grassy hillsides, sheltered valleys and moors dance with the insects when the sun shines, but immediately it goes behind a cloud they all disappear. They will only be tempted to fly in dull weather if the air is very warm.

The slug-like caterpillars feed on grass by night, and readily fall from the stems and 'play dead' if disturbed. They live about ten months compared to about three weeks for the butterfly. The Scotch argus, which was once known as the northern brown, used to occur in several upland counties of northern England, but is now extinct there.

Notes and Sketches

A dark brown butterfly with buff patches. Each fore-wing has a false eye with a white centre, and each hind-wing has three false eyes. The female has larger buff spots than the male, with slightly rounded wingtips. Wingspan 1¾ in. (45 mm).

There are two to four generations a year. Caterpillars of the early summer become fully grown in about a month. Autumn caterpillars live through the winter, feeding during warm spells, and take eight or nine months to become fully grown.

Male

Female

Large buff spots

Widespread in the south and in Ireland; an isolated population in Scotland.

SITES GUIDE

This butterfly will defend a sunny position against intruders. It tends to be a creature of habit and may be spotted in the same place for several days. Speckled woods are very common and may be seen at many of the woodland sites in this book including 2–4, 6, 7, 9–11, 13–16, 18, 19, 21–29, 31, 34–36, 45, 46, 49–53, 56, 57, 60.

Speckled wood *Pararge aegeria*

In the 18th century this butterfly became known as the Enfield eye when it was identified in rural Middlesex. Today it is a familiar butterfly of suburban parks, commons and the rough areas of golf courses. It is also a resident of southern English woodlands. Its speckled wings give it ideal camouflage in the dappled world of light and dark where sunlight percolates through the canopy and scatters over brambles and honeysuckle. It can be seen, as well, around woodland margins, along paths and hedgerows, and in clearings. Its spots and connection with woods gave it another 18th-century name, wood argus, after the many-eyed hero of Greek mythology. In the west of England and Wales the speckled wood can be found in more open habitats of hillsides and cliffs.

The butterflies exhibit a high degree of territorial behaviour, establishing themselves in sunny glades which they defend and where they conduct their courtship. The amount of speckling on the wings varies from region to region and season to season. Four sub-species occur – in Scotland, the Isles of Scilly, southern England and Snowdonia, each one with different wing patterns. Males that hatch in autumn are darker than those in spring.

Notes and Sketches

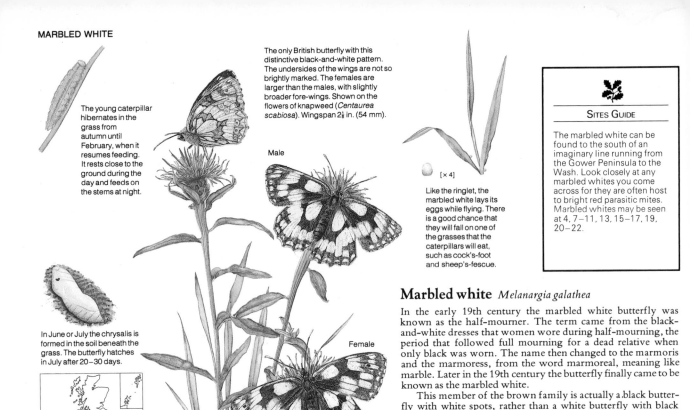

The young caterpillar hibernates in the grass from autumn until February, when it resumes feeding. It rests close to the ground during the day and feeds on the stems at night.

The only British butterfly with this distinctive black-and-white pattern. The undersides of the wings are not so brightly marked. The females are larger than the males, with slightly broader fore-wings. Shown on the flowers of knapweed (*Centaurea scabiosa*). Wingspan 2⅛ in. (54 mm).

Male

[× 4]

Like the ringlet, the marbled white lays its eggs while flying. There is a good chance that they will fall on one of the grasses that the caterpillars will eat, such as cock's-foot and sheep's-fescue.

In June or July the chrysalis is formed in the soil beneath the grass. The butterfly hatches in July after 20–30 days.

Found mostly in the south of Britain, but can occur as far north as York.

Female

SITES GUIDE

The marbled white can be found to the south of an imaginary line running from the Gower Peninsula to the Wash. Look closely at any marbled whites you come across for they are often host to bright red parasitic mites. Marbled whites may be seen at 4, 7–11, 13, 15–17, 19, 20–22.

Marbled white *Melanargia galathea*

In the early 19th century the marbled white butterfly was known as the half-mourner. The term came from the black-and-white dresses that women wore during half-mourning, the period that followed full mourning for a dead relative when only black was worn. The name then changed to the marmoris and the marmoress, from the word marmoreal, meaning like marble. Later in the 19th century the butterfly finally came to be known as the marbled white.

This member of the brown family is actually a black butterfly with white spots, rather than a white butterfly with black spots. However the black-and-white wing patterns sometimes vary, and it may occasionally look as though it belongs to the white-butterfly family. Its most common breeding grounds are chalky downland slopes, but it also exploits Forestry Commission paths on chalk soil, open grassy wastelands, moors and damp meadows. In its favourite locations the butterfly can be extremely abundant in July and August. It feeds on flowers with the wings open, showing off the bright contrasting colours which are probably a visual deterrent to predatory birds. Knapweeds and scabious are favourite nectar sources.

Notes and Sketches

The white eggs are laid singly on various species of grass and hatch after about 17 days. [× 4]

White-centred spots

The chrysalis is formed in a shallow chamber in the soil, and the butterfly hatches in June or July.

Found along the coast of Britain, particularly in the south and the west.

The caterpillar feeds on different grasses, including couch (*Agropyron repens*). It lives through the winter, feeding during mild spells.

A powerful flyer that will not stay still to be examined closely. When it comes to rest on flowers it always closes its wings, showing two black spots with white centres. Wingspan up to 2 in. (50 mm).

SITES GUIDE

While the marbled white may be the odd one out of the 'browns' in terms of coloration, the grayling is quite different in its lifestyle. Its chrysalis is formed in an underground chamber rather than hanging from a grass stem. The grayling is a coastal species and it may be seen at 1, 7, 9, 10, 19–21, 27, 28, 30, 42, 44–46, 48, 51, 53, 54, 60, 63, 64.

Grayling *Hipparchia semele*

Britain's largest brown butterfly, with its silver-grey underside, shares its common name of grayling with a freshwater fish of a similar colour. It is mostly a coastal butterfly, living on the grassy slopes and hollows at the top of cliffs. It is also found on the chalky downs, the heathlands of the New Forest and the grasslands of Salisbury Plain. But it is not at all common. The old name of the Tunbridge grayling refers to a time when it flew in the Weald of Kent near Tunbridge Wells, where it no longer exists.

The butterfly is an expert in concealment. When landing after swift, but very short flights, it tilts over sideways to the sun so as not to cast an obvious shadow. It often settles on stony or earthy ground where – after it retracts its fore-wings between the hind-wings – its underside coloration blends into the background. The false eyes on both sides of the wings are found throughout the brown family, and are used to confuse predatory birds as to the position of the head. Graylings rarely visit wild flowers for nectar, but they are believed to drink sap from oak and pine trees. There are six sub-species, including a small one on Great Orme Head in North Wales.

Notes and Sketches

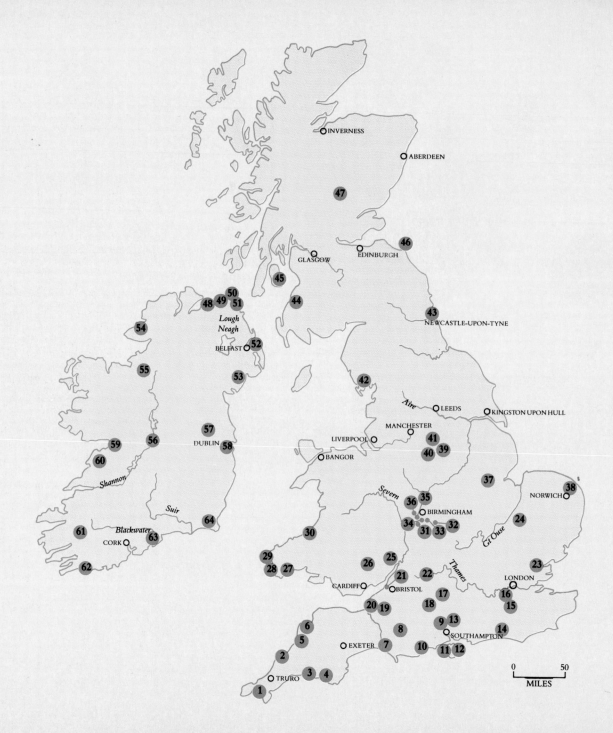

INVERNESS

○ ABERDEEN

47

46

45

GLASGOW ○   EDINBURGH

44

50
48 49 51

54

*Lough
Neagh*

43
NEWCASTLE-UPON-TYNE

BELFAST ○ 52

55

53

42

Aire

57

59   56

○ LEEDS

○ KINGSTON UPON HULL

DUBLIN   58

LIVERPOOL   MANCHESTER

60

○ BANGOR

41
40   39

Shannon

37

38
NORWICH ○

Severn

36 35

24

Suir

34
31 33 32

BIRMINGHAM

Blackwater

61   63

64

Gt Ouse

CORK ○

62

30

29
28   27

26

25

23

21

22

Thames

LONDON ○

CARDIFF ○   BRISTOL ○

16

20 19

18

17

15

6

8

9 13

14

5

○ EXETER

7

10

SOUTHAMPTON

2

11 12

3   4

TRURO ○

1

0   50

MILES

The sites

Here is a gazetteer of sites in England, Wales, Scotland, Northern Ireland and the Republic of Ireland where you may see the species listed on pages 12–95. Sites in England, Wales and Northern Ireland are managed by the National Trust, those in Scotland by the National Trust for Scotland, and some of the sites managed by An Taisce are among those listed for the Republic of Ireland.

The order in which the sites are arranged on the following pages corresponds to the numbers on the map opposite. The gazetteer starts with the southernmost location in England and ends in the south-eastern corner of the Republic of Ireland. For ease of reference, there are three main sections: England and Wales, Scotland, and Ireland. Each section is preceded by an additional map, showing the sites relevant to that part of the country. So, if you are living in or visiting the south of England, for example, you will be able to select those sites which are nearest your area.

The dots on the map are intended to give only a rough guide to each location. Each individual site entry will tell you which county the site is in and will give you more precise instructions on how to reach the property you wish to visit. Where applicable, opening times and admission fees are given and, of course, there is information on which species you may expect to see at the site.

Many of the places included in this book form part of the grounds of historic houses which are also open to the public. If you are interested in visiting the houses as well as their grounds and need further details of their opening times during the year and entry fees, check with your local tourist office.

English and Welsh sites

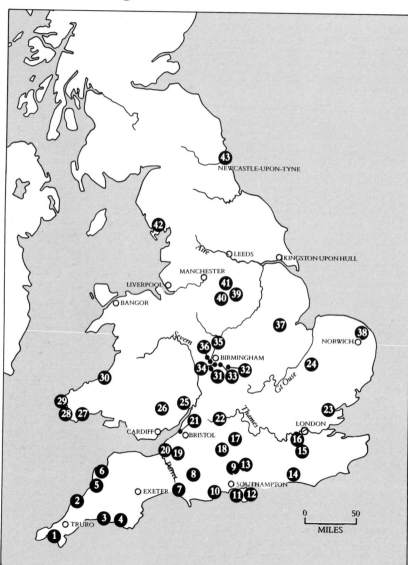

LOCATION *Cornwall*; **1 mile south-west of Ashton, halfway between Helston and Marazion.**

The 33 acres at Rinsey Cliff contain a diversity of habitat types, the most widespread of which is gorse scrub with some patches of blackthorn. The gorse is one of the food plants of the larvae of the green hairstreak butterfly and this insect may be seen in places. Although locally common throughout much of Britain, especially in the south, it is only sparsely distributed in Cornwall and its presence here is important for the Cornish population of the green hairstreak.

Maritime grassland on the cliff edge and on the cliff itself includes a variety of food plant species such as restharrow and bird's-foot-trefoil which are favoured by the caterpillars of the common blue. It has been noted in the past that this butterfly is particularly abundant here, and may be seen together with small heath and large skipper.

The old quarry on this site is also worth investigating. It provides significant shelter in what is an exposed situation and large whites and large skippers have been observed here. Look out, too, for orange tip, grayling, small copper and small skipper, all of which you should see.

---

2   PARK HEAD

LOCATION *St Eval, Cornwall*; **6 miles south-west of Padstow.**

Anyone who knows Bedruthan Steps on the north Cornish coast will have seen Park Head, because this is the large rocky headland which forms the background to the view from the steps. A mosaic of habitats can be found on the property – which is over 200 acres in extent. The unenclosed areas around the cliff tops are covered with grassland and grass heath, while some of the side valleys support scrub, marshy areas and in some parts even a few trees.

The best places to look for butterflies are on the grass and heath areas, especially the slopes above Porth Mear. Those with larvae feeding on grasses and nettles such as small heaths, ringlets, red admirals and painted ladies are frequent, along with common blues and dark green fritillaries.

Park Head is a site with stone faced 'hedges' typical of Cornwall. These frequently have a rich flora and provide sunny aspects and warm shelter beloved by butterflies. Look out for large skippers here. Large whites, speckled woods and small tortoiseshells also occur.

3   PENCARROW HEAD

LOCATION *Cornwall*; at the west end of Lantivet Bay, 2 miles east of Fowey, between Polruan and Polperro.

Pencarrow Head is one of the most distinctive landmarks in the south Cornish coastline. The views from the Head are exceptional – you can see Rame Head and Bolt Tail to the east and the Dodman and the Lizard to the west.

The property itself is large and it encompasses a variety of different habitats. Below the improved grasslands along the cliff top – where the fields are grazed by sheep and cattle – are a number of steep pastures which have escaped improvement. These are herb-rich, lightly grazed, largely south-facing and so attract various

butterflies such as the common blue. The cliff-top paths through the cliff slopes have their margins mown to keep back the bracken, and these are also attractive areas for butterflies which enjoy the shelter of the margins. Small coppers have been observed here and you should be able to find them without too much difficulty.

Perhaps the best sites for butterflies are the woodlands. These are not mature and therefore have little high canopy. They are scrubby with clearings and a rich sinuous edge. Here you may find comma butterflies which are only locally abundant in Cornwall.

Other species you may see at Pencarrow Head are small tortoiseshell, ringlet, clouded yellow, meadow brown, gatekeeper, large skipper, speckled wood, wall, small white and, among the aristocrat butterflies, red admiral, painted lady and peacock.

4   POLPERRO

LOCATION *Cornwall*; 3 miles southwest of Looe on the A387.

The National Trust landholdings at Polperro lie on either side of the harbour mouth. The vegetation is varied and consists of a patchwork of scrub, bracken and grassland with maritime grassland on the cliffs and cliff edges. Old lanes and streams add further interest, along with old allotments which are now mostly abandoned. Those which are still cultivated probably provide food for small whites which are to be found here.

The coarse grassland areas with their sheltered patches of scrub are rewarding places to search for butterflies and species such as the small skipper, gatekeeper and meadow brown are characteristic. Some

of the old lanes and pathways provide sheltered corridors which are favoured by flying insects and butterflies.

Species you may see here include small tortoiseshell, small copper, marbled white, large skipper and speckled wood.

5   MAER CLIFF

LOCATION *Bude, Cornwall*; immediately adjoining the town, running north to Northcott Mouth for $\frac{2}{3}$ mile.

Maer Cliff is frequently used by visitors to gain access to the beach at Bude and other small coves in the area. The pastures along the cliff are crossed by a coastal footpath so trampling feet and heavy grazing keep the cliff-top grasses short. As a result the best places to seek butterflies here are around some of the typical Cornish hedgebanks with their core of stones and soil surmounted by hazel and other shrubby species. These give shelter and warmth as well as providing a habitat for many food plants. You may see meadow brown, gatekeeper, wall, common blue and large white here.

The gatekeeper in particular is a lover of the sun-traps that these banked hedges provide, giving rise to its common name – the hedge brown. Wall browns, too, like the warmth but should you see any basking in the sunshine, approach them quietly or they will be inclined to fly off and settle further down the trail.

6   PENTIRE HEAD

LOCATION *Cornwall*; about 1 mile north of Polzeath, 6 miles north-west of Wadebridge – approach by the B3314.

Pentire Head is a blocky headland protruding from the north Cornwall coast to the east of the mouth of the River Camel. Butterflies are found here in the varied cliff-top grassland and grass heath plant communities, which occur between the edge of the farmland and the cliffs themselves. The most interesting sites are along the western side of the very exposed Pentire Head, the Rumps Point area and near Doyden Castle and Epphaven Cove.

The grasslands are varied because of a number of factors. The differences in underlying geology, the degree of exposure and the depth of soil all play their part, although the influence of aspect – especially the salt deposition that it brings – is most obvious. The number and variety of plants in these herb-rich grasslands has a profound effect on the butterfly population and several species may be found here. The presence of bird's-foot-trefoil will encourage the common blue, for example, because it is the food plant of its caterpillar. You should also spot some of those butterflies which have grass-feeding larvae, such as ringlet, small heath, meadow brown, gatekeeper, large skipper and small skipper.

Other species which you may observe are small tortoiseshell, small copper, speckled wood, large white, small white and painted lady – a well known migrant. The females of this species sometimes arrive on British shores – after a journey through north-west Europe – with an abdomen full of eggs which they will lay here in the grassland along the cliffs.

7   GOLDEN CAP

LOCATION *Dorset*; 4 miles east of Lyme Regis across Lyme Bay; about 3 miles south-west of Bridport. Access via the A35 from Morcombelake and Chideock.

This huge estate of more than 2,000 acres contains some of the highest cliffs in southern England – you can gain access to them along the coastal footpath. Much of the site, especially the cliff and hill areas, is open to the public and there are over 15 miles of pathways. The estate lies almost entirely within the West Dorset Heritage Coast and most of the coastline, including the cliffs and undercliffs, is a designated Site of Special Scientific Interest.

A number of the woodland areas contain butterfly populations but the best places for good sightings of a variety of species are on the hilltops and cliffs. These tend to be covered with a rich mosaic of heath, scrub and acidic grassland, while dwarf shrub heath of heather, gorse and bracken occurs in limited patches. Fritillaries have been seen here along with the small heath which, although not limited to heathland, seems to prosper in this area.

Other butterflies recorded at Golden Cap include: small tortoiseshell, orange tip, ringlet, holly blue, painted lady, dingy skipper, brimstone, grayling, peacock, small copper, wall brown, meadow brown, marbled white, speckled wood, large white, green-veined white, small white, gatekeeper, small skipper and red admiral.

You may also see the common blue in the area. Males of the common blue have been observed drinking from patches of animal excreta – helping them to gain the vital minerals they require to make insect hormones. They will even settle on human skin to drink salt-rich sweat.

8   WIN GREEN HILL

LOCATION *Wiltshire*; 5 miles south-east of Shaftesbury, ½ mile north-east of the B3081.

Excellent views can be had from the top of Win Green Hill, which rises to over 900 feet and is one of the highest points in the county. An old trackway known as the Ox Drove crosses the summit plateau and it is here, in the chalk grassland, that various butterflies may be found. The south-east facing slopes have also proved fruitful in the past and marbled white, ringlet, small heath and gatekeeper have been seen. Look out too for small skipper, small tortoiseshell, painted lady, meadow brown and red admiral. Dark green fritillaries have also been noted in this part of Wiltshire.

9   KINGSTON LACY

LOCATION *Dorset*; 2 miles north-west of Wimborne, to the west of the B3082.

The Kingston Lacy estate fits neatly into the confluence of the Rivers Stour and Allen and these watercourses form the estate boundaries for some considerable distance. There are a number of small woods on the estate which have a limited number of butterfly populations. The oak and hazel woodland of Abbott Street Copse contains speckled wood butterflies – these are often seen in sunny clearings – while some of the damper woodland areas and alder copses are attractive to brimstones and small, large and green-veined whites. Red admirals, speckled woods and green-veined whites have been seen in the woodlands within the parkland itself and it is worth inspecting areas where nettles grow.

This estate is best known, however, for the presence of Badbury Rings – an Iron Age hill fort with Bronze Age burial mounds – which is a popular destination for many visitors every year. Its semi-natural chalk downland vegetation includes calcareous grassland, scrub and scrub woodland and a vast number of plant species can be found here.

The chalk turf, facing different directions at different angles and in sheltered positions, has also resulted in an enormous variety of butterfly habitats. The soil of these downland areas tends to favour chalk-loving wild flowers such as marjoram, thyme, vetches, knapweeds, scabious and yellow carline thistles. From these, butterflies can reap a harvest of nectar, particularly in the warm hollows and on the slopes facing south.

The woodland is dominated by pine and has a useful ground flora of nettles and brambles, and with blackthorn, hazel and gorse around the fringes.

The list of butterflies that have been seen here is great. Of the commoner species, small skipper, large skipper, dingy skipper, grizzled skipper, orange tip, green hairstreak, purple hairstreak, small copper, brown argus, common blue, holly blue, small tortoiseshell, peacock, comma, wall, marbled white, grayling, small heath, ringlet, gatekeeper and meadow brown are known to occur.

Meadow browns and gatekeepers are both butterflies which make great use of woodland clearings and may also be seen along hedgerows and ditches.

10 BROWNSEA ISLAND

LOCATION *Dorset*; reached by ferry from Poole Quay and Sandbanks. Visitors may land their own boats at the Pottery Pier at the west end of the island.
OPEN 28 Mar to 27 Sept; daily 10–8 or dusk if earlier.
ADMISSION Landing fee £1; parties 70p by written arrangement with the Warden.

A visit to Brownsea Island is full of excitement with a boat trip across Poole Harbour and the thrill of exploration when you arrive. No wonder it was the location for the first Boy Scout camp – arranged by Baden Powell in 1907. There is a large slab of Portland stone on the island which commemorates the experiment. When the weather is clear, there are magnificent views over the Dorset coast. Standing on the southern cliffs, looking out over Poole Harbour, you may be able to see the ruins of Corfe Castle, which nestles in a cleft between the Purbeck Hills. Almost the whole of the northern half is a nature reserve of some 200 acres managed by the Dorset Trust for Nature Conservation who allow access by means of guided walks at set times in the summer. The reserve has one of the largest heronries in England and attracts a wealth of wildlife, including sea birds such as terns and Canada geese. A salt-marsh and lagoons on the island also provide sanctuaries for the wildfowl.

The rest of the island is largely pine and birch woodland with some areas of acidic grassland and heath, as well as the coastline of low cliffs and beaches. The tall pines form an open woodland into which sunshine penetrates on fine days to attract insects with its warmth.

The butterflies here are impressive. The grassland areas are worth searching for large skippers and brown argus while ringlets may be found in the damper areas and flying along woodland glades. Other skipper butterflies to look for include the small skipper and the dingy skipper. The caterpillar of the dingy skipper has only one food plant, the bird's-foot-trefoil. While the adult butterflies will visit the flowers for nectar, they are unlikely to benefit the plant by bringing about pollination – this calls for insects such as bees or wasps which are heavier, and strong enough to force pollen from the joined lower petals.

Butterflies of Pieridae family – whites and yellows – are represented on the island by brimstones, large whites, small whites, green-veined whites and orange tips. Other species that you are likely to see here are small copper, common blue, holly blue, small tortoiseshell, peacock, comma, speckled wood, wall brown, marbled white, grayling, gatekeeper, meadow brown, small heath, painted lady and red admiral.

The red admiral is one of the butterflies which feeds on nettles and benefits by having chosen a food plant that is both common and widespread in Britain and Europe – a particular advantage for migrant butterflies. The stinging hairs of the nettle also contrive to protect the butterfly – they have the advantage of discouraging many grazing animals which would otherwise eat the eggs or caterpillars as they fed on the plants. The painted lady also feeds on nettles, but its main food plant is the thistle, whose prickles serve the same purpose as the hairs of the nettles in deterring grazers.

11 NEWTOWN

LOCATION *Isle of Wight*; **5 miles west of Newport, 1 mile north of the A3054.**

The Newtown River occupies a ria – a naturally flooded river valley – on the coast midway between Cowes and Yarmouth. The National Trust site includes all its many branches which add up to 14 miles of river estuary, together with a number of small woods, about 40 acres of fields and an area of salt marshes. Most of the property is a Site of Special Scientific Interest and this biological value has been further recognised by its designation as a Local Nature Reserve in 1965.

The best areas to look for butterflies are in the woodlands of which there are almost 90 acres. These are dominated by oak, in the canopy of which are a diversity of insects including the purple hairstreak butterfly. The woods, which contain an excellent variety of native trees and shrubs including ash, field maple and hazel together with aspen, hornbeam, spindle and guelder rose, are well broken up with rides. Some of these are broad, open and sunny almost like clearings and attract sun-seeking butterflies, while others are narrower and more shaded and are favoured by species like speckled wood.

The fields on this site are rich in plants. These, along with brambly hedgerows, make particularly good butterfly habitats and marbled whites and common blues may be seen here. The coarse grassland by the town hall and its neighbouring pond is also worth inspecting – a good variety of butterflies have been observed here including gatekeeper, meadow brown, small skipper and small copper.

Other species to look for at Newtown include brimstone, large white, small white, green-veined white, holly blue, small tortoiseshell, peacock, wall, red admiral and painted lady.

12 BEMBRIDGE AND CULVER DOWNS

LOCATION *Isle of Wight*; **over 100 acres on the east of the island, to the south-west of the village of Bembridge, which is 4 miles south-east of Ryde.**

These two adjacent properties, with their fine sea views, lie on the narrow chalk ridge which runs east-west across the Isle of Wight. The underlying strata are almost vertical and finally emerge in the Needles at the extreme western tip of the island. At Culver Cliff the land drops away very steeply and provides many nesting sites for sea birds.

Both areas have been grazed consistently during the past 20 years and those parts where the sward is shortest are least good for butterflies. In fact, the best butterfly sites are outside the grazing land altogether, on the ungrazed fringe of cliff-top grassland and on those parts of the cliffs where landslips have occurred in the past and which contain heathland species of grass favoured by butterflies.

Painted ladies have been observed in the more sheltered locations provided by the scrub on the northern cliffs and this site may be the first landfall for many of these butterflies during their spring migration from southern Europe and North Africa. You may also see dingy skippers, large whites, small whites, brown arguses, peacocks, wall browns, gatekeepers, meadow browns, small heaths, common blues and small tortoiseshells which have been seen in the area in the past.

13 SELBORNE HILL

LOCATION *Hampshire*; **4 miles south of Alton, between Selborne and Newton Valence, west of the B3006.**

Selborne is well known for its historical connections with Gilbert White who recorded his wildlife observations in *The Natural History and Antiquities of Selborne*. Selborne Hill rises to the south-west of the village to a height of over 600 feet. It is common land and is covered mainly with beech and oak woodland, some of it growing on the very steep chalk hillside immediately above the village. This area, known as the Hanger, is one of Hampshire's most interesting woodlands and has been designated a Site of Special Scientific Interest. Gilbert White's writings have made the area particularly valuable for historical ecologists who are able to compare the site as described by White in the 18th century with today's woodland.

The beech trees are well mixed with other tree species such as ash, field maple and yew in the hanging woods and with oak and ash on the more acid plateau. The woodland flowers here are also very varied and this encourages butterflies.

On the plateau itself is a clearing of semi-natural grassland surrounded by various scrub species including blackthorn, holly and elder and containing a pond. Here, too, are butterflies such as the marbled white and dingy skipper. Species to look out for at Selborne include small skipper, large skipper, grizzled skipper, brimstone, large white, small white, green-veined white, orange tip, green hairstreak, small copper, common blue, holly blue, small tortoiseshell, peacock, comma, red admiral, painted lady, speckled wood, wall, gatekeeper, meadow brown, small heath and ringlet.

14   HIGHDOWN HILL

LOCATION *West Sussex*; 1 mile north of Ferring, 3 miles north-west of Worthing, 1 mile south of the A27, between the South Downs and the sea.

This hill is an outlier of the South Downs. It is only about 2 miles from the sea and the views from it are very attractive. The banks of an ancient hill fort are apparent on its slopes and, not surprisingly, its archaeological importance is enormous. Iron Age and Bronze Age remains have been found here together with a Saxon cemetery.

A variety of butterflies may be seen here including the brown argus, the caterpillars of which generally feed on rock rose and also hibernate on it.

The common rock-rose is not in fact a rose at all but a wild flower which typically grows on scrub, grassland and in rocky places. It has small buttercup-yellow petals and very hairy leaves.

Look out for large whites, green-veined whites, small whites, small tortoiseshells, red admirals, painted ladies, small coppers, common blues, gatekeepers, meadow browns, speckled woods, small heaths and wall browns.

15   BOX HILL

LOCATION *Surrey*; 1 mile north of Dorking, 2½ miles south of Leatherhead, east of the A24, close to Burford Bridge.
OPEN All year. Pay and Display car/coach parks at top of hill.

Box Hill is a prominent feature of the North Downs escarpment. This prominence is partly because it rises to over 600 feet and partly because the River Mole – following its course northwards to the Thames – runs immediately to the west of the property, cutting into the rounded contours of the escarpment and exposing its chalk side to create a dramatic river-cut cliff.

The downland and woodland vegetation here provide habitats full of biological interest which is recognised by the designation of much of the Box Hill area as a Site of Special Scientific Interest. It is also acknowledged that this is one of the best butterfly sites in the ownership of the National Trust and entomologists are asked to contact the Trust in order to co-ordinate as much information about the butterfly interest of the area as possible to assist with their management programme.

The Box Hill property contains a good range of woodland types including beech woods and yew woods on the steep chalk slopes, mixed beech and oak woods on the clay plateau and scrub woodland development in various stages in several locations. These wooded areas are home for many butterflies typical of the habitat. Purple hairstreaks are common in the canopy of the oaks while a choice of broad sunny rides and shaded paths attract other species. White admiral and pearl-bordered fritillary have been observed in this area in the past.

In common with many other members of the fritillary family, the pearl-bordered fritillary is a violet feeder. Its caterpillar – black with yellow spines – favours woodland violets. After hibernation it will revive in spring to feed on the leaves of species like the sweet violet. The sweet violet is the only violet which has scented flowers and is considered the easiest to recognise. Pansies, too, are members of the violet family but apart from these, there are about nine species of violet in Britain.

Unfortunately, the dependence of the pearl-bordered fritillary on one type of food plant could endanger its survival. Violets tend to grow in the shade of woodland and are often found in coppice woods. Coppicing is a way of encouraging a tree to sprout long straight shoots, which are then harvested and used for fencing poles and other agricultural purposes. The decline of the practice has resulted in a number of coppice woodlands being destroyed completely to make way for arable land, and this has contributed to the steady loss of violet food plants. On the brighter side, the decline of this kind of woodland benefits another species – the white admiral, by encouraging the growth of the only food plant of its caterpillar – honeysuckle.

The chalk downland areas are generally rich in grassland plant species and where these have scrub margins they become considerably enhanced as suitable habitat for butterflies. The Lower Viewpoint, Dukes and Juniper Top are all three worth investigating. Small skippers and several species of blue are known to occur here together with Essex skipper and green hairstreak. You should also explore Lodge Hill which is thought by many to be the best site for butterflies on Box Hill.

You may also see large skipper, dingy skipper, grizzled skipper, brimstone, large white, small white, green-veined white, small copper, brown argus, small tortoiseshell, peacock, comma, speckled wood, marbled white, common blue, chalk-hill blue and holly blue.

Both the holly blue and the common blue produce two generations a year. While caterpillars of the common blue will feed on a variety of members of the pea family, those of the holly blue feed only on holly in spring and ivy in autumn.

16 RANMORE COMMON

LOCATION *Surrey*; **2 miles north-west of Dorking adjoining the south boundary of the Polesden Lacey estate.**

Ranmore Common covers almost 500 acres of the chalk North Downs. Although located on the northern slopes, the ground drops gently away in a series of spurs and parallel dry combes which join an east-west running dry combe before rising again to Polesden Lacey House. The Common consists of two main areas. The eastern portion is well wooded with a mixture of mature trees and is a designated Site of Special Scientific Interest; the area to the west is old heathland, now growing a mixture of birch and bracken.

The most abundant trees are beech and these are found mostly on the valley sides and also mixed with oaks on the ridges. Many other tree and shrub species can be found here growing beside the beech and oaks, including holly, cherry, crab apple, blackthorn, whitebeam, spindle and privet. Buddleia also occurs locally and its attraction to butterflies is well known. The woodland ride system with both open sunny sections and shaded parts is an important habitat.

There is a splendid variety of woodland butterflies to look for. Purple hairstreaks live in the oak canopy while white admirals and dark green fritillaries have been recorded on the North Downs and may possibly be seen on this site by the keen observer. The rides are especially rewarding and marbled whites, meadow browns, ringlets and commas are some of the species which have been seen along them. Other species you should look for are small skipper, large skipper, brimstone, large white, small white, green-veined white, orange tip, common blue,

brown argus, small tortoiseshell, red admiral, painted lady, peacock, speckled wood, wall brown, gatekeeper and small heath.

17 CHERHILL DOWN

LOCATION *Wiltshire*; **on the A4 between Calne and Beckhampton.**

Cherhill Down is part of the Calstone and Cherhill Site of Special Scientific Interest which includes one of the best networks of deep dry valley coombes on chalk in Britain. The National Trust land lies in the northern part and although it includes neither the White Horse nor the monument, it does have an Iron Age fort.

The western spur is the best area for butterflies. Here, the deep valleys have steep slopes with a variety of aspects and these encourage a very rich grassland community with a wide diversity of associated flowers. Both these factors attract an exciting list of butterflies, the marbled white among them. This butterfly lays its eggs in grassland and two grass species upon which its caterpillars feed, cock's-foot and cat's-tail, occur. These plants are sufficiently common for the marbled white to have evolved what might seem a high-risk method of distributing its eggs – the butterfly scatters them over the grassland during flight. Other species to look out for are: small skipper, large skipper, dingy skipper, brimstone, large white, small white, green-veined white, brown argus, common blue, small tortoiseshell, peacock, wall brown, gatekeeper, meadow brown, small heath, ringlet and painted lady. The chalk-hill blue and the dark green fritillary have been found in the general area in the past.

18 RAINBOW WOOD FARM

LOCATION *Avon*; **on Claverton Down, 1 mile south-east of Bath.**

Good views can be obtained from this site, although access is limited to public footpaths. In spite of its large size, most of this property is under arable cultivation and only small areas are of biological interest. Rainbow Wood itself may be of ancient origin. It is mainly beech woodland with some oak and a dense understorey of hawthorn, hazel, holly, cherry and yew. Speckled woods have been recorded here.

To the west of the wood are four meadows rich in their variety of wild flowers. Some of these are on steep slopes and those that face west hold good numbers of feeding butterflies in fine weather. Look out for meadow browns, common blues, small tortoiseshells, large skippers and painted ladies.

19 CHEDDAR CLIFFS

LOCATION *Somerset*; **8 miles north-west of Wells. Roadside parking at Black Rock Gate on the B3135 at the south-west corner of the property; public footpath.**

With over two million visitors a year, the dramatic gorge at Cheddar, with its sheer soaring cliffs, is well known to many. Less well known, though, are the surrounding woodlands and grasslands which are owned by the National Trust and which contain a wealth of butterflies. The large areas of permanent grassland are rich in plant species and thus provide food for a wide variety of caterpillars. Much of the area is south-facing and the shrubs and thickets to be found here create warm sheltered pockets even on cool days.

There are plenty of docks and sorrel to feed the larvae of the delightful small copper while the warm slopes and prolific clovers and trefoils are irresistible to clouded yellows in a good year. You may also observe large skipper, dingy skipper, brimstone, large white, small white, green-veined white, orange tip, brown argus, common blue, holly blue, small tortoiseshell, peacock, comma, speckled wood, wall, marbled white, grayling, gatekeeper, meadow brown, small heath, ringlet, painted lady and red admiral.

20   BREAN DOWN

LOCATION *Somerset*; the south arm of Weston Bay, 2 miles south-west of Weston-super-Mare.

A western extension of the Mendips, Brean Down is one of three promontories along with Worlebury Hill and Sand Point which push out into the grey waters of the Bristol Channel. It is covered with a mixture of dense scrub and open grassland while the sides of scree and bare cliffs drop steeply to the sea below. The grassland in the open areas is sheltered by scrub of hawthorn, bramble and ash trees, severely stunted by the winds which blow from the Atlantic. These are favourable areas for many species although, on fine days, graylings seem to prefer the grassy south-facing slopes.

Look out for small heaths, brimstones, wall browns, meadow browns, marbled whites, large whites, small whites, common blues, gatekeepers, red admirals and painted ladies. Chalk-hill blues and dark green fritillaries have been seen along this coast of Somerset in the past.

21 MIDDLE HOPE AND SAND POINT

LOCATION *Avon*; 5 miles north of Weston-super-Mare.

S and Point is the northernmost of the three parallel promontories projecting into the Bristol Channel from the Avon and Somerset coast. Its mixture of scrub and calcareous grassland supports a wide range of butterflies. Middle Hope, which has a north-facing shoreline, consists largely of pasture fields and lies to the east of Sand Point.

The thick scrub on the point provides sheltered areas of grassland which attract many butterflies, especially in these exposed coastal locations, and the presence of rock roses are an added bonus for the brown argus whose caterpillars feed on this plant. Other butterflies here include small skipper, dingy skipper, brimstone, large white, green-veined white, small white, orange tip, small copper, common blue, holly blue, small tortoiseshell, comma, red admiral, painted lady, wall, marbled white, grayling, gatekeeper, meadow brown and speckled wood.

22   FROCESTER HILL

LOCATION *Gloucestershire*; near Nympsfield between Stroud and Dursley on the B4066.

A t the northern end of Coaley Wood and crossed by the Cotswold Way, lies Frocester Hill, which consists of a mixture of woodland and scrub, grassland and a disused quarry face. It is one of the reserves of the Gloucestershire Trust for Nature Conservation, and while it is protected mainly for its botanical and

geological interest, it also has a good selection of butterflies. These favour the steep south-westerly sloping grasslands and species such as the common blue and the small skipper are found here. The common blue lays its eggs singly on plants which are members of the pea family, such as bird's-foot-trefoil, restharrow or clover. Look for the caterpillars in June and August, and again from September to April.

The males and females of the common blue display different colours, that is, they are sexually dimorphic. This indicates that butterflies can see colours. Indeed, the range of colours they perceive is far greater than that of humans – they can see ultraviolet light as a colour. The petals of some plants both absorb and reflect ultraviolet light and form patterns invisible to the human eye, but which attract nectar-seeking insects to the plant.

Look out, too, for brimstone, large white, small white, green-veined white, small copper, painted lady, peacock, red admiral, small tortoiseshell, gatekeeper, marbled white, meadow brown, ringlet, small heath, speckled wood and wall.

23   BLAKE'S WOOD

LOCATION *Essex*; **5 miles east of Chelmsford, just south-west of Little Baddow.**

The National Trust owns 105 acres of deciduous woodland on the western slope of the ridge running southwards from Little Baddow to Danbury. This is a nature reserve managed by the Essex Naturalists' Trust and is part of a Site of Special Scientific Interest.

The tree species here are mostly sweet chestnut and hornbeam coppice, together with hazel. Streams run through the wood creating wet clearings and these, along with the open rides and paths, are attractive to butterflies. Meadow browns and gatekeepers are both butterflies which make great use of such woodland clearings and may be seen here. Speckled woods have recently started to colonise this part of Essex and these, too, may be spotted on this site.

Other species recorded here include peacock, large white, green-veined white, comma and red admiral.

24   WICKEN FEN

LOCATION *Cambridgeshire*; **3 miles west of Soham, 17 miles north-east of Cambridge via the A10.**
OPEN All year: daily except Christmas Day.
ADMISSION £1; parties 75p by arrangement with the Warden.

Over 600 acres of the original Great Fen of East Anglia are preserved at Wicken where the National Trust have acquired the four fens which make up this property. The site has been designated a Site of Special Scientific Interest by the Nature Conservancy Council and is one of the oldest nature reserves in Britain. It has been popular with naturalists for over a century – the Victorians used to come here by train to collect flowers, insects and even birds.

Sedge grows in great quantity and has been harvested for thatching for more than 500 years. This cutting of the sedge is also favourable to milk parsley, food plant of the larvae of the swallowtail butterfly which used to breed here. Unfortunately, the local population of this beautiful insect died out in about 1950 and swallowtails are no longer seen at Wicken Fen.

Some of the most promising places to look for butterflies on this site are in the droves. These are mown access tracks cut through the fen and many flowers grow along them. But for this mowing regime, they would quickly revert to reed beds and sedge fields. Their rich flora attracts insects and you may find brimstones, holly blues and orange tips. Another excellent spot to see butterflies is at the entrance to the fen where buddleia bushes have been planted beside the William H. Thorpe building. In flower, they attract peacocks, commas, red admirals, small tortoiseshells and painted ladies.

The list of butterflies recorded at Wicken Fen is impressive and you may also see large white, small white, green-veined white, meadow brown, ringlet, gatekeeper, small heath, speckled wood, wall, green hairstreak, dingy skipper, small skipper, Essex skipper, small copper and common blue.

Blue and copper males usually display larger amounts of metallic colour on their wings than the females. The duller colouring of the females helps them to avoid predators and lay their eggs in safety. Some females of the blues are brown.

25   MAY HILL

LOCATION *Gloucestershire*; **9 miles west of Gloucester, 1 mile north of the A40.**

May Hill stands on the western side of the Severn Plain and rises to almost 1,000 feet. From the top there are extremely good views and, on a clear day, you can see ten counties from here.

The best sites for butterflies are on May Hill itself where the summit vegetation consists of dry acidic grassland and the slopes are covered with a mixture of dwarf shrubs and bracken. Several species have been noted here, including small copper, small heath and common blue.

Lower down the slopes are two areas of woodland. Bearfoot Wood is a larch woodland and speckled wood butterflies have been found here. Other species you may see include green-veined white, green hairstreak and holly blue.

26   BETTWS NEWYDD

LOCATION *Gwent*; **4 miles north of Usk, 4 miles west of Raglan.**

Fine views can be obtained from the summit of this hill fort around which the River Usk winds on its way to the sea. The woodland growing on the steeply sloping earthern ramparts is mostly abandoned 'coppice with standards', but only a few mature oaks – the standard trees, allowed to grow and become large – are to be found among the spindly beech, ash, birch and sweet chestnuts which are the remains of the outgrown coppice.

The density of the tree canopy discourages most butterflies except in sunspots, particularly on the footpaths, where speckled woods may be seen. The summit of bracken and grassland is sufficiently sheltered in parts to attract other butterfly species and both meadow browns and ringlets are common here.

27 STACKPOLE WARREN

LOCATION *Dyfed*; 4 miles south of Pembroke. Access over public and other marked footpaths. Car parks at Stackpole Quay and Broadhaven.

Stackpole is a large property situated within the Pembrokeshire Coast National Park. It consists of a number of different elements including limestone and old red sandstone cliffs with grassland and scrub vegetation, three deep lakes dammed during the last century at Bosherton, areas of sand dunes and farmland containing isolated fragments of woodland. Bosherton Lakes and Stackpole Warren, the area of dunes to the north-west of Stackpole Head, are managed by the Nature Conservancy Council as a National Nature Reserve.

One of the most promising sites to look for butterflies at Stackpole is in the coarse grassland, especially on the cliffs at Trewent Point where a dozen species have been recorded in the past including green hairstreak and grayling.

You should also find butterflies among the dune systems at Broad Haven and at Gupton and Brownhill Burrows. The larvae of the brown argus feed on stork's-bill which grows in the grey dune areas and, as a result, the butterfly is locally common.

You may see other species such as painted lady, small skipper, large white, green-veined white, small white, common blue, wall brown, speckled wood, large skipper, peacock, gatekeeper, meadow brown, small copper, small heath, ringlet and small tortoiseshell.

28 MARLOES, ST BRIDE'S BAY

LOCATION *Dyfed*; 7 miles west of Milford Haven, at the south end of St Bride's Bay.

Pushing out into the sea to the south of St Bride's Bay is the Marloes peninsula. From here there are good views to both Skokholm and Skomer Islands and across the bay towards Ramsey Island and St David's. The property falls within the Pembrokeshire Coast National Park and there is a long distance coastal path running through it.

The peninsula encompasses a number of aspects and exposures – ranging from the very exposed cliffs facing south-west to more sheltered northern areas and parts which face south-east. The length of coastline here totals almost 3 miles and the habitats include scrub, coarse grassland and grass heath.

The best area for butterflies is the maritime grassland especially where it grows on south-facing slopes. Typically the common blue is abundant while small copper, small heath and wall brown may also be seen. Other species which may be observed are small skipper, large skipper, large white, small white, green-veined white, orange tip, green hairstreak, red admiral, painted lady, small tortoiseshell, peacock, speckled wood, grayling, gatekeeper, meadow brown and ringlet. The dark colours of the meadow brown and the ringlet help them to camouflage themselves in the long grass. (Black and brown colours are caused by melanin.)

29 ST BRIDE'S BAY

LOCATION *Dyfed*; west-facing bay stretching from Ramsey Sound in the north to Skomer in the south and to Rickets Head in the east.

St Bride's Bay is a large and diverse National Trust property. Linear in form, it follows the coastline and includes scrub, grassland, maritime grassland, heath and a very small amount of woodland. The maritime grassland contains many flowering species typical of this habitat and a number of butterflies have been noted here, especially those whose caterpillars can find food plants locally. Small heaths and wall browns are two examples of butterflies whose larvae are grass feeders and they may be seen here.

Wetlands are the other major areas where you may find butterflies at St Bride's Bay. Although not a significant feature, the stream valleys leading to the sea have an established community of waterside plants. Some of these are tall species, such as angelica, which provide food for butterflies, and green-veined whites and orange tips may be observed here. The orange tip is one of the butterflies in the Pieridae family – the whites and yellows – which displays territorial behaviour. Look for this butterfly patrolling the margins of woodland, and along hedgerows and ditches.

Look out, too, for the following species: small tortoiseshell, ringlet, small copper, meadow brown, gatekeeper, large skipper, speckled wood, large white, small white, common blue, small skipper, painted lady and peacock. The peacock's eye-catching display of colour – together with the false eyes – gives a warning to potential predators. Bright colours often indicate that an insect is poisonous.

30 LOCHTYN

LOCATION *Dyfed*; rocky headland 1 mile north of Llangranog, 6 miles south-west of New Quay.

The views from this shoe-shaped promontory – especially from Pen-y-Badell, the hill here that rises to almost 500 feet – are splendid and encompass the whole coast of Cardigan Bay. There is a wide variety of habitats including grassland, scrub heath, bracken, woodland and rocky crags.

The scrub areas provide some of the best butterfly habitats on this site because they supply the shelter so necessary in such an exposed maritime situation. The most rewarding areas to search, however, are the mosaic of ridges and gullies along the south-western coastal strip. These not only contain damp grassland in the dips but also tall herbs which are sought by feeding butterflies.

Look out for peacocks, graylings and wall browns – all of which are common on this property.

31 HANBURY HALL

LOCATION *Hereford and Worcester*; 2½ miles east of Droitwich, 1 mile north of the B4090, 6 miles south of Bromsgrove.
OPEN Apr and Oct: Sat and Sun and Bank Hol Mon 2–5; May to Sept: Wed to Sun and Bank Hol Mon 2–6.
ADMISSION £1.60. Pre-arranged parties of 15 or more £1.10. Free car and coach park.

Hanbury Hall was built at the beginning of the 18th century and it is probable that the present park was laid out

at the same time. However, the area is also the site of a medieval deer park which originally belonged to the Bishops of Worcester. The age of some of the trees in the grounds reflects this, and the oldest specimens have a girth of up to 18 feet.

Much of the grassland, especially that to the south of the road, has been improved for agricultural purposes and consists mainly of rye grass species. The best areas are on the gentle slopes to the north of the property where there is permanent pasture rich in its diversity of flowers and grasses.

Small skippers may be found here feeding on thistles and knapweed or laying their eggs on soft grass. You may also see common blue, large white, green-veined white, large skipper, orange tip, peacock, small copper, small heath, speckled wood and wall brown.

32 BADDESLEY CLINTON

LOCATION *Warwickshire*; ¾ mile west of the A41 Warwick to Birmingham road, near Chadwick End, 6 miles north of Warwick, 11 miles south-east of central Birmingham.
OPEN Apr to end Sept: Wed to Sun and Bank Hol Mon 2–6; Oct: Sat and Sun 12.30–4.
ADMISSION £1.80; reduced rates for parties by prior arrangement with the Administrator. Free car park and coach park.

The 120 acres of Baddesley Clinton encompass a variety of woodland and pasture, together with a number of pools and ponds. The insect life of the water areas is enriched by the proximity of the Grand Union Canal, which passes very close to the western boundary of the estate, while the woods consist of a mixture of

species including native ash and oak.

The best place to see butterflies is in the wildflower area of the garden where the grass is allowed to grow until August, each year, before it is cut. Up to eleven species have been recorded here at one time including the gatekeeper which is attracted by the long grasses on which its caterpillars feed. You may also see large whites, green-veined whites, small whites, orange tips, small coppers, common blues, red admirals, painted ladies, peacocks, wall browns and meadow browns.

33 PACKWOOD HOUSE

LOCATION *Lapworth, Warwickshire*; about 1½ miles east of Hockley Heath (on the A34), 11 miles south-east of central Birmingham.
OPEN Apr to end Sept: Wed to Sun and Bank Hol Mon (closed Good Fri), Oct: Sat and Sun 12.30–4.
ADMISSION £1.60. Pre-arranged parties of 15 or more £1.10. Free car park and coach park.

Packwood House, which partly dates from Tudor times, stands in over 100 acres of parkland. The park is divided by a minor road and each half consists of open parkland, grazed by stock, with ponds and woods. It was once the deer park of the Prior of Coventry but by the 18th century the area had been broken up into fields. Today's redeveloped parkland is therefore comparatively modern.

Although the woodland areas may shelter species such as the gatekeeper, the best areas for butterflies are the open grasslands, especially that known as The Paddock to the south of the house, where common blue, meadow brown and green-veined white have been recorded.

34 GROVELEY DINGLE

LOCATION *Hereford and Worcester*; at the south edge of Birmingham, on the east side of the A441.

Groveley Dingle comprises a number of steep-sided stream valleys leading to a feeder reservoir for the Worcester and Birmingham Canal, an arm of which actually enters the south-eastern corner of the property.

A greater part of the woodland here is well over one hundred years old and has been designated a Site of Special Scientific Interest. It is managed by the Worcestershire Nature Conservation Trust to whom application should be made for a permit for access.

The age of the woodland is indicated by the variety of its shrub layer which includes dogwood, guelder rose and holly. Also present are brambles and nettles and, as a result, the comma butterfly has frequently been seen here. This butterfly likes to establish its territories along hedgerows and in secluded corners. The markings on the underside of the comma are dull, concealing the butterfly when it rests with its wings closed. When the wings are open, they display the comma's bright colours which attract members of its own species, and therefore encourage mating encounters.

Apart from the woodland, the Dingle contains pastureland, some of it unimproved where the slopes are steep, and this helps to encourage a wide diversity of butterflies. Among those to be seen here are small tortoiseshell, peacock, orange tip, brimstone, large white, green-veined white, small white, ringlet, small heath, meadow brown, speckled wood, small copper, common blue, small skipper and large skipper.

35 CHADWICH MANOR ESTATE

LOCATION *Hereford and Worcester*; 4 miles north of Bromsgrove, at the south-west edge of Birmingham, astride the A38 road to Worcester. Access only by public footpath except at Highfield where there is a country park.

This estate is a complex mosaic of land uses comprising 432 acres of woodland, arable and improved pastureland, unimproved grazing and ponds with surrounding wetland areas. Almost as complicated are the various forms of management. There are ancient woodlands which have been designated Sites of Special Scientific Interest and are managed by the Worcestershire Nature Conservation Trust, farmland managed by the Bournville Village Trust and a country park at Waseley Hill looked after by the County Council. From Highfield there are fine views of the Malvern Hills.

Such a diversity of habitats ensures that a wide variety of butterfly species should be seen here on fine days. Look out for speckled wood, meadow brown, red admiral, small tortoiseshell, comma and peacock. The striking colours of the peacock are intended to frighten away predators, as are the false eyes on its wings, which imitate the shape of an animal's eye. If the butterfly is disturbed it will open and close its wings rapidly to enhance the startling effect of its warning.

You may also see common blue, holly blue, large white, green-veined white, small white, orange tip and brimstone.

In the meadow areas, keep an eye out for the small skipper. Skipper butterflies are usually very swift flyers, so are sometimes difficult to spot in flight.

36 CLENT HILLS

LOCATION *Hereford and Worcester*; 3 miles south of Stourbridge, south-east of Hagley, north and east of the village of Clent.

This property consists of two major hills, Clent Hill and Walton Hill, which rise to over 1,000 feet. From their tops are fine views west and north-westwards to Clee Hill and The Wrekin in Shropshire and southwards to the Malvern range.

Both hills are common land and their acidic soil produces a typical vegetation of grassland, heath and bracken. Their lower slopes are more wooded with a wide variety of tree species. Where the ground is well drained, oak predominates while in the wetter areas it is joined by sycamore and birch. These trees, and the hawthorn scrub which grows with them, have grown up since grazing ceased during the 1930s. The valley between the hills, the Clatterbach Valley, has more enclosed woodland as well as grazing land.

The open commons are rewarding areas to search for butterflies – orange tips, in particular, have been noted here in the early summer.

Another member of the whites that you should have many opportunities to observe is the small white – a very common butterfly. One particular characteristic of the females while resting is that they will raise their abdomen to signal to the males that they do not wish to mate.

Other species include ringlet, small heath, meadow brown, speckled wood, wall brown, large white, green-veined white, peacock, red admiral, painted lady, common blue, small copper, holly blue, small skipper, comma, small white and large skipper.

| 37 | BELTON PARK |

LOCATION *Grantham, Lincolnshire*; 3 miles north-east of Grantham on the A607 Grantham to Lincoln road.
OPEN All year; access on foot only from the Lion Gates. Park may be closed for special events.

Belton Park slopes gently down to the River Witham which flows through its grounds. It was laid out as parkland in the 18th century and much of the area is now used as pasture.

Although there has been some agricultural improvement, visible evidence of the old ridge and furrow suggests that the grass is certainly long established in parts. Like the golf course, which has been in use since 1892, these areas of old grassland are rich in their plant varieties, which attract butterflies.

The best areas have proved to be around the old lily pond alongside the River Witham where tall stands of willowherb entice large white butterflies to feed on their nectar.

Large whites and other members of the whites have evolved an efficient deterrent against the lizards and birds which might prey on them – poison. They obtain sulphurous compounds from the cabbage leaves on which their caterpillars feed. These are called mustard oil glycosides, the taste of which will deter most predators. Although the glycosides in cabbage are not poisonous to humans, they are responsible for the unpleasant smell of the vegetable when it is cooking.

Keen observers may also see small skippers, small coppers, common blues, small tortoiseshells, green-veined whites, small whites, orange tips, brimstones, ringlets, gatekeepers and meadow browns.

| 38 | BLICKLING HALL |

LOCATION *Norfolk*; 1½ miles north-west of Aylsham, 15 miles north of Norwich, 10 miles south of Cromer on the north side of the B1354.
OPEN 11 Apr to 1 Nov: daily except Mon and Thur but open Bank Hol Mon 1–5; closed Good Fri.
ADMISSION Garden £1.50; house £2.50; pre-booked parties £2.00.

The Blickling Estate, which covers almost 5,000 acres, is a lowland agricultural estate used mainly for intensive arable farming with some 600 acres managed for forestry purposes. As a result, the butterfly interest tends to be very localised and is largely restricted to a few good habitats.

Ringlets and meadow browns have been spotted in and around the woodlands on the estate, and the vegetation round some of the ponds may be attractive to butterflies.

It may be worth searching Abel Heath and the adjacent disused railway line. Here the deep railway cutting provides both shelter and a good aspect to the sun. This, together with open grassland and the well drained nature of the site, has made it popular with a rich variety of butterflies including the small heath. The small heath tends to be abundant along roadsides and ditches, as well as on grasslands, but even this common butterfly can be affected by changes to habitat caused by man. When rabbits were introduced to the British Isles, many butterfly species benefited from the effects of the grazing, which produced the same result as regular mowing. The grazing kept down the coarse grasses and produced the kind of habitats on which butterflies such as the small heath and large blue thrive. However,

when myxomatosis was introduced to keep down an overwhelming rabbit population, the situation was reversed. Grassland was overtaken by scrub and woodland and the small heath died out in some areas.

| 39 | HARDWICK HALL |

LOCATION *Derbyshire*; 6½ miles north-west of Mansfield; 9½ miles south-east of Chesterfield.
OPEN Park open daily throughout the year.
ADMISSION Car park charge to non National Trust members 40p.

This extremely large area of parkland was originally laid out in Elizabethan times and contains many relics of its history and development since. The western part of the estate is now managed as a country park to which there is full access.

The River Doe Lea runs through the park just inside the western boundary and its passage is marked by a series of ponds together with the remains of an old duck decoy. Butterflies are often abundant around these ponds and various whites, browns and some members of the skipper family have been noted here.

Tree planting has been carried out around the old duck decoy where there is also a dense undergrowth with willow and fen vegetation and a variety of mature trees. This mosaic of habitats is most attractive to butterflies, especially in the clearings where meadow browns, commas, peacocks and small skippers have been observed. In addition to these, you may see large whites, small heaths, common blues, small coppers, large skippers, green-veined whites and nettle-feeding small tortoiseshells.

40 DOVEDALE

LOCATION *Derbyshire*; **4–7 miles north-west of Ashbourne, west of the A515. Access by footpath.**

Dovedale lies to the south of the Peak District National Park and is well known for its scenic beauty and wildlife importance. Not surprisingly it has been designated a Site of Special Scientific Interest. The River Dove flows through the bottom of the valley from the sides of which tall limestone spires and pinnacles rise through thick ash woodland.

Interspersed with the woodland are flower-rich grasslands. Well drained and south-facing, they attract a variety of insects including a host of butterflies. Milldale is of particular interest because the brimstones which occur here are at the northern edge of their range in the Dovedale area. The following have also been recorded here: dingy skipper, small white, green-veined white, orange tip, common blue, small tortoiseshell, peacock, small heath and red admiral.

Grizzled skipper and green hairstreak have occasionally been seen in the area in the past.

41 LONGSHAW

LOCATION *Derbyshire*; **1–3 miles south-east of Hathersage, on the south side of the A625. OPEN All year.**

The Longshaw estate is a well-wooded area on the west-facing millstone grit escarpment which drops quite steeply down to the River Derwent at Grindleford. Much of the 1,100 acres forms Longshaw Country Park and part, Padley

Woods, is designated a Site of Special Scientific Interest. The woods occupy the narrow steep-sided valley of the Burbage Brook and their interest lies mainly in the semi-natural sessile oak woodland which has survived here. This, and Bolehill Wood which falls into the same SSSI, contain a number of butterfly species – small tortoiseshell, small skipper, meadow brown and comma have all been seen here. The clearings and areas of dappled shade are worth searching.

Butterflies are also found in the open areas of dwarf-shrub heath at Lawrence Field which lies above Burbage Brook. Here dwarf shrubs, such as bilberry and crowberry, are mixed with moorland grasses and attract species with grass-feeding larvae such as meadow brown and large skipper.

Other butterflies you may observe around the Longshaw estate are red admiral, painted lady, peacock, brimstone, large white, orange tip, small white, small heath, wall brown, common blue, green-veined white and green hairstreak.

42 SANDSCALE HAWS

LOCATION *Cumbria*; **3 miles north of Barrow-in-Furness, 3 miles west of Dalton, on the A595.**

Sandscale Haws is an area of sand dunes and slacks on the south side of the Duddon Estuary. They extend to almost 700 acres and vary from mobile dunes close to the seashore to more stable dunes further inland. This is an ever-changing habitat with colonising plants stabilising and enriching the sand and allowing other species to follow them. Between the dunes are slacks or hollows. Some remain dry throughout the year, others flood in the

winter, while others are always wet and support marsh plants.

A good variety of butterflies is common and typically includes the small copper, small heath and the grayling which particularly loves maritime habitats. You should also look out for small tortoiseshell, dingy skipper, meadow brown, large skipper, large white, small white, green-veined white, common blue, red admiral and painted lady.

43 NEWTON LINKS

LOCATION *Northumberland*; **55 acres of sand dunes and rough grazing south of Long Nanny in Beadnell Bay, which is 2 miles south of Seahouses.**

Lying to the south of Beadnell village, Beadnell Bay is one of those long and empty sandy beaches for which Northumberland is famous. Long Nanny Burn joins Brunton Burn just before they enter the North Sea, and Newton Links lies to the south of this small estuary.

Most of the property consists of sand dunes, some stabilised, where hardy seashore plants like marram grass are well established and hold the dunes in place, and some growing or shrinking as a result of wind and wave action.

Marram is a coarse species of grass which will withstand salt and wind but is not particularly appealing to grass-loving butterflies. However, plants more suited to grass-feeders like small heath and meadow brown will colonise the stabilised dunes. A variety of other species may be seen here including large white, small white, green-veined white, common blue, red admiral, small tortoiseshell, small copper and painted lady.

Scottish sites

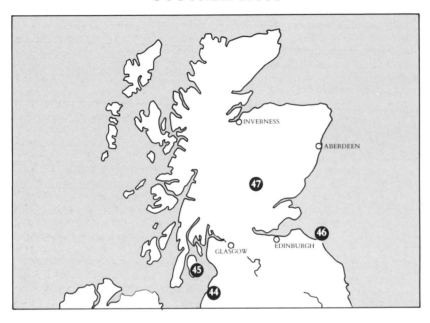

44 CULZEAN COUNTRY PARK

LOCATION *Strathclyde*; **4 miles west of Maybole.**

Culzean was given the status of Country Park in 1969 and was the first so designated in Scotland. It consists of an estate of 560 acres with 2½ miles of rocky coastline. There is an impressive range of habitats here including 290 acres of mixed woodland, dune and heathland, grassland and salt and fresh water. In addition to these, there are extensive gardens.

Although there are pure stands of conifers on the estate, much of the woodland is mixed with wide sunny rides and over 17 miles of paths. The shelter provided by the trees together with the warmth in the clearings are enjoyed by butterflies. One of the best places on this property to search for these insects is in the gardens. These were laid out to provide shelter from the sea winds in this exposed location and will attract butterflies for this reason.

In particular, there is a beautiful walled garden with a wide range of cultivated plants together with a transitional area, known as Happy Valley, between the formal and informal parts of the estate. Look out for white butterflies in these parts, together with aristocrat butterflies such as small tortoiseshells, peacocks and red admirals.

Other species you may see include dingy skippers, large white, small white, green-veined white, brimstone, orange tip, painted lady, common blue, small copper, meadow brown and small heath.

You may also see grayling here – a butterfly which exploits several different species of grass for food, laying its eggs on marram grass in dune areas or on sheep's fescue, a plant which favours chalky soil.

45 BRODICK COUNTRY PARK

LOCATION *Strathclyde*; **on the south-east coast of the Isle of Arran.**

This Country Park lies on the south-eastern coast of the Isle of Arran. Although only 170 acres in extent, it contains a variety of habitats including woodlands of various kinds together with rough grazing, sandy and rocky shores and gardens which all provide plenty of opportunity for seeing butterflies. Behind the Country Park, the National Trust for Scotland owns a further 7,300 acres which takes in the well known Goatfell.

The property contains extensive gardens which enjoy a mild climate as a result of the island's westerly maritime location. This if further enhanced in the walled garden and this factor, together with the range of plants growing here, is attractive to butterflies. Look for orange tips, painted ladies and peacocks here.

Elsewhere in the Country Park, the mixed and deciduous woodlands supply sheltered areas most important to butterflies which try to avoid sea winds. There are rides and paths through these and you may see speckled woods and meadow browns.

Other species recorded at Brodick include large white, small white, green-veined white, small tortoiseshell, red admiral, common blue, small heath, ringlet, wall, grayling, green hairstreak, purple hairstreak and small copper. These last three species are all from the Lycaenidae family of butterflies, some of whose members have evolved an effective disguise to protect themselves from predators. They mimic their own head and antennae by displaying tails and eye-spots on their hind-wings.

46 ST ABB'S HEAD

LOCATION *Borders*; **rocky headland about 1 mile north of St Abbs.**

This coastal property, covering almost 200 acres, has been declared a National Nature Reserve by the Nature Conservancy Council. Closely grazed grassland covers the majority of the reserve, although there are areas of gorse scrub and rough grass around the man-made Mire Loch. This is a deep glaciated valley which has been dammed and then flooded.

The property has an impressive list of breeding and visiting butterflies and many of their caterpillars' food plants grow here. There are sheltered south-facing slopes too and these always attract sun-seeking butterflies. The grayling is commonly found along coastlines especially in the west. So although it is quite expected here, where the sea is so close, it is found much less frequently on the eastern seaboard. Look for it along the lighthouse road from Petticowick Bay. This butterfly is an expert at blending in with its surroundings, and adapts its colouring to match the areas where it settles. In chalk areas, therefore, the grayling frequently appears in a light-coloured form.

Ringlets which are near the northern edge of their range also occur on the reserve and can be seen on fine summer days in the grasses of the Mire valley especially in the wet areas. These butterflies will also fly in damp weather.

You should look out, too, for large white, small white, green-veined white, orange tip, speckled wood, meadow brown, red admiral, painted lady, peacock, small tortoiseshell, small copper and common blue.

47 LINN OF TUMMEL, THE PASS OF KILLIECRANKIE AND CRAIGOWER HILL

LOCATION *Tayside*; **south-east of Atholl along the A9.**

The National Trust for Scotland's Pass of Killiecrankie property is joined directly to the Linn of Tummel by a footbridge, while Craigower Hill overlooks them both. The three areas provide a variety of habitats for butterflies. At the Linn of Tummel there is a fine area of mixed woodland where Scots pine, Douglas fir and larch grow alongside ash, alder, beech, sycamore and oak. Gaps in the tree canopy allow sunlight to filter through and in these clearings you may come across butterflies such as the small copper, the small heath and the orange tip.

Across the River Garry, the mixed woodlands of the Pass of Killiecrankie line the narrow rocky gorge through which the river pours its peaty brown waters. On this side of the river, small tortoiseshells, red admirals and the beautiful Scotch argus have been recorded, the last being almost totally confined to Scotland. Look for it on sunny days, for on dull ones it remains hidden in the grasses.

A variety of butterfly species also occurs on Craigower Hill, an old beacon which rises to 1,300 feet and from which are beautiful views particularly to the west when Loch Rannoch is visible on fine days. The flowers on the hill are very attractive to butterflies and, as buddleia grows here, you may expect to see small tortoiseshells and common blues clustering around it when it is in bloom. You should also see large white, small white, green-veined white, dark green fritillary, green hairstreak and meadow brown.

Irish sites

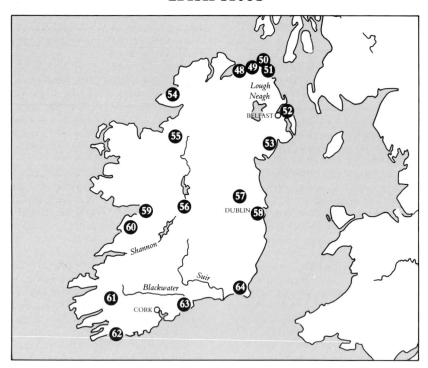

Lough
Neagh

BELFAST

Shannon

DUBLIN

Suir

Blackwater

CORK

LOCATION *Co Londonderry*; **a 3-mile stretch of duneland to the west of Portstewart.**

This property is well known for its variety of butterflies. It consists of a dune system forming a spit $1\frac{1}{2}$ miles long projecting north of the River Bann estuary. The area they cover in the ownership of the National Trust extends to almost 200 acres. The Trust also owns about 25 acres on the west bank of the river opposite the Portstewart Dunes.

The dunes themselves are dominated by large blocks of scrub, consisting mainly of sea buckthorn. This is not a native of Ireland but has been widely planted on the dunes in the past to help to stabilise the sand. It forms a very spiny and impenetrably dense scrub which can prove difficult to control.

There are different types of dune here – ranging from embryo dunes, through mobile yellow dunes to fixed grey dunes, amongst which are dune slacks. The fixed dunes have a covering of dune grassland. Often in habitats of this type, such grassland is kept as short tuft by rabbit-grazing but here the rabbits do not seem to have recovered very quickly from myxomatosis and the grass is long and rank as a result. The small heath is especially common here but many other species have also been recorded including red admiral, common blue, small white, green-veined white, large white, meadow brown, small copper, wall, grayling, painted lady, and small tortoiseshell. Small coppers and blues – often seen flying together – are easy to spot because of their bright, metallic colours. These are caused by tiny corrugations on the surface of their wing scales which refract the light.

49 WHITE PARK BAY

LOCATION *Co Antrim*; **7 miles north-west of Ballycastle.**

This is a fine sandy bay on the north coast flanked by high chalk cliffs. There have been some rock falls and slippage in the past leaving both chalk scree and large blocks and boulders which have become covered with vegetation. Inland lie grassland and scrub woodland. The scrub grows only in the less exposed areas and comprises elder, hawthorn, blackthorn and gorse in a tangle of bramble. It provides much needed shelter for butterflies and speckled wood and wood white have been recorded here. The wood white – a delicate butterfly which is scarce in England, Wales and Scotland – frequents scrub and open woodland and is locally common in Ireland.

Inland of White Park Bay is a narrow band of dunes supporting a fairly diverse dune vegetation with characteristic plants able to withstand dry conditions. Such areas are favoured by common blues and small heaths both of which are common in this area.

A variety of butterflies has been noted here including orange tip, small copper, small tortoiseshell, meadow brown, large white and green-veined white.

50 LARRYBANE AND CARRICK-A-REDE

LOCATION *Co Antrim*; **coastal site 5 miles west of Ballycastle, off the B15.**

These two properties cover an area of almost 90 acres and lie on the beautiful and geologically varied northern coast. Although separate, they are no great

distance apart and are linked by the Fisherman's Path. In the summer, a visit to Carrick-a-Rede is made more exciting because of the 60-foot-long rope bridge erected 75 feet above the water to link the island with the mainland.

The major features of this area are the tall chalk and basalt cliffs inland of which are pasture and patches of scrub. Some of the pasture is in the form of terraced fields divided by steep banks which are used as rough grazing. Much of this and the cliff grassland contains heathland species favoured by butterflies.

You may find small tortoiseshell, orange tip, peacock, small copper, speckled wood, large white, green-veined white, small white and common blue butterflies here.

51 FAIRHEAD AND MURLOUGH BAY

LOCATION *Co Antrim*; **3 miles east of Ballycastle.**

There is an enormous variety of habitats to be found in this 764-acre property. As its name suggests, it is a coastal site in one of the most beautiful areas of this part of Ireland. In addition to the coastline itself, the area contains heathland and acid grassland, three small lakes, limestone grassland and woodlands in the shelter of Murlough Bay.

Of the woodlands, the Birch Wood, consisting largely of downy birch with substantial amounts of rowan and hazel, is the best for butterflies. It is on the steep northern and eastern slopes which drop down to the sea at Murlough Bay and so is screened from the prevailing wind – although the amount of sunshine the wood receives is limited. You may see speckled

woods and orange tips in this area together with wood whites. These frail butterflies are scarce in England, Wales and Scotland but are locally abundant in Ireland.

The geology of this area is very complex and gives rise to the variety of grassland types. These are favoured by several species of butterfly and the small heath, in particular, is common. Look out, too, for small tortoiseshell, ringlet, grayling, peacock, small copper, meadow brown, green-veined white, common blue and red admiral.

52 BALLYMACORMICK POINT

LOCATION *Co Down*; **about 3 miles north-east of Bangor.**

This property lies on the southern coast of the north of Belfast Lough. Its maritime situation adds to its biological interest and increases the variety of habitats. At the same time, it does limit the amount of woodland except in the most sheltered areas.

Scrub thrives here and dominates most of the Point running down almost to the sea in the less exposed parts. Gorse and bramble are the main species but on the seaward side there is a strip of maritime grassland and heath, especially where the soils are shallow and the ground rocky. Typical butterflies to be found in these dry grassland areas are common blue, small heath and wall brown.

There is also some freshwater seepage across the Point to the sea and green flushes are a frequent feature. Lusher grasses grow here and attract butterflies like the ringlet, orange tip and green-veined white. Other species found on the Point include meadow brown, large white, small white and speckled wood.

53 MOURNE COASTAL PATH

LOCATION *Co Down*; **running south of Newcastle, along the coast.**

The Mourne Coastal Path runs northwards between the sea and the Mountains of Mourne before turning inland to follow the Bloody Bridge Valley, which is a gorge cut by a fast-flowing spate river. The shoreline here consists of rock and boulders behind which are low boulder-clay cliffs which are cut in a number of places by valleys carrying water to the sea.

Much of the property is covered with thickets of gorse, hawthorn and bramble, together with an abundance of bracken. The most interesting areas for butterflies, however, are along the sides of the Bloody Bridge River where there are sweeps of dry grassland and heath, a habitat rare in the north of Ireland. Here, a variety of species have been observed including the grayling, which can frequently be found in coastal areas.

Other species to look out for include small tortoiseshell, speckled wood, meadow brown, small copper, wall, peacock, small heath and green hairstreak.

54 LOUGH SHESKINMORE

LOCATION *Co Donegal*; **about 4 miles north of Ardara.**

The lough is cut off from Loughros More Bay by an extensive sand dune system on its south and west sides. Wild flowers in profusion grow on the low marshy margins of the lough, including several rare orchid species. On the north side, where there is access to the lake from a narrow lane, the ground rises rapidly in rocky, heatherclad hills. The area is not only noted for butterflies, but for the barnacle and white-fronted geese which winter here on an Irish Wildbird Conservancy reserve.

The orange tip may be seen on the damp ground leading down to the lough, while the sand dunes shelter dingy skippers, small and common blues, dark green fritillaries, walls and graylings. Green-veined whites, wood whites, small coppers, small heaths, meadow browns, ringlets and small tortoiseshells are more widespread.

Outside the immediate lake environment, the green hairstreak is usually abundant, although there can be great fluctuations in numbers from year to year. In south-west Donegal look for widespread populations of large heath in the boggy areas which blanket so much of the region.

55 SLISH WOOD

LOCATION *Co Sligo*; **about 5 miles south-east of Sligo on the south side of Lough Gill.**

At the bottom of the wood, which covers the steep western slope of Killerry Mountain, a stream runs northeast towards the lake. On the gentler eastern slopes, the high rocky moorland changes to wet bog lower down. The oaks along the edge of the stream provide a perfect environment for the purple hairstreak and this is the farthest north in Ireland the insect has been observed.

In early summer, the woodland edge of the stream is the best place to see wood whites, dingy skippers and orange tips – all butterflies which prefer rough ground. In midsummer, meadow browns and ringlets may be seen, giving way to small tortoiseshells, peacocks and red admirals in late summer. Look for large, small and green-veined whites in both early and late summer. The broad-leaved woodlands around Lough Gill are good sites for holly blues and silver-washed fritillaries. On the eastern slopes of the mountain, you may see green hairstreaks sunning themselves on the rocks.

56 MONGAN BOG

LOCATION *Co Offaly*; **on the north side of Fin Lough, between Ballynahown on the N62, and the ruined monastery of Clonmacnoise.**

Mongan is one of the very few examples in Ireland of a raised bog. Apart from one or two small areas of exploitation on its eastern end and north-western fringes, it is intact, a great 320-acre convex spread of heathery moorland, whose conservation is under the care of An Taisce.

During high summer, favoured areas of the bog are alive with large heath, while the green hairstreak and wood white haunt its busy margins earlier in the year. The brimstone also is a frequent visitor. Hawthorn, whitebeam, dogwood and spindle are among the typical woodland trees and shrubs which provide vantage points for the green hairstreak. This butterfly is territorial and will quickly establish areas which it defends against encroachment by other insects. The flowered areas of the eskers (ridges of limestone gravel) which lie to the north and south-east should yield common blues, dingy skippers, large whites, orange tips, small coppers, red admirals, small tortoiseshells, peacocks, speckled woods and meadow browns.

57   THE BOG OF ALLEN

LOCATION *Prosperous, Co Kildare*; 22 miles west of Dublin on the L2. Bog and marshland areas north of the village.

The easternmost fringes of the great Bog of Allen penetrate fertile farmlands to the north of Prosperous. These low-lying swampy areas, together with clumps of gorse by the roadside, provide ideal habitats for a number of butterfly species. Green hairstreaks abound in the gorse while marsh fritillaries and large heaths prefer the boggy areas. The caterpillars of the marsh fritillary protect themselves from predators and winter weather by spinning silk into a specially thickened communal web, in which they will hibernate. In the spring, they emerge from the web and individual caterpillars will bask on leaves in the sunshine. Their jet-black colouring enables them to absorb and retain warmth from the sun's rays. The marsh fritillary is one of the many species endangered by the activities of man. The drainage and cultivation for agriculture of the wetland regions they frequent deprive them of favourable habitats.

Around the Ballynafagh Reservoir you should also catch sight of the green hairstreaks and the comparatively rare dingy skippers, wood whites and brimstones. Dark green fritillaries may suddenly appear almost anywhere in the entire area during their respective flight seasons.

Look out too for the more common butterflies such as large, small and green-veined whites, small coppers, small tortoiseshells, speckled woods, walls, meadow browns and ringlets. The dark colours of the meadow brown and the ringlet help these butterflies to camouflage themselves in the long grass.

58 THE GLEN OF THE DOWNS

LOCATION *Co Wicklow*; a steeply sloping valley with wooded sides, 18 miles south of Dublin off the N11.

Melt waters from Ice Age glaciers cut this large, striking V-shaped valley, which is forested with oak trees, and lower down its slopes, holly trees. Hollies grow in abundance on the west side of the valley, and in May you should be able to see holly blues among their foliage. Other early butterflies include the orange tip and wood white which can be seen around the woodland edges near the valley stream.

The wood white makes a habit of patrolling hedgerows and clearings. These butterflies can be seen on the wing for long periods, even though they are not strong fliers. One of the reasons for this behaviour is that the female takes great care in selecting suitable food plants on which to lay her eggs. Female butterflies fly in close to plants to touch them briefly with their feet. The receptors in the foot enable the butterfly to analyse quickly the chemical composition of a plant and decide whether it is the right species.

Whites are succeeded in late June by meadow browns and ringlets, but the insect population is richest in August. At this time you may catch sight of purple hairstreaks on the wing around the north-west corners of the glen, although they can be difficult to spot. The valley stream runs through sheltered areas of grass and flowers, disappearing into a culvert under the road at the south end. In August, the buddleias which grow here are not only a favourite haunt of painted ladies, but also of peacocks, red admirals and small tortoiseshells. You may also see some late browns and second generation whites.

59   CLARINBRIDGE

LOCATION *Co Galway*; 8 miles south-east of Galway on the N18.
ADMISSION Obtain permission from the Christian Brothers who run the house.

On the east side of the road through the village lies the entrance to Kilcornan. If you carefully cross the dry-stone wall on the north side of the drive, you will enter a field just west of a belt of conifers. The field is rough pasture, bounded by the Clarinbridge River on the north. The profusion of wild flowers and the blackthorn scrub that encroaches on the wood from the east make this site attractive to numerous species of butterfly. Blackthorn is also known as the sloe, from the small blue-black fruits it bears. The wood of this shrub is hard and tough and is often used for making walking sticks – the Irish shillelagh, or cudgel, is traditionally made from the wood of the blackthorn. Brown hairstreaks lay their eggs on the leaves of the sloe which will eventually be food for the caterpillars.

Clarinbridge is famous in the annals of Irish entomological history as being the site at which brown hairstreaks were first discovered in the mid 19th century. The insects are still here and are most easily seen in early September, although they can be difficult to find. Even if your search for the brown hairstreak is unsuccessful, you should not be disappointed because the knapweed, scabious and ragwort in the field attract small tortoiseshells, red admirals, peacocks, silver-washed fritillaries, large whites and meadow browns, with some brimstones, small coppers, walls, common blues and painted ladies. In early summer look for wood whites, dingy skippers and holly blues.

60   THE BURREN

LOCATION *Co Clare*; **immediately south of Galway Bay. Bare limestone hills lying between the N67 and the N18.**

An Taisce owns 39 acres of land just east of Gortlecka and a large area around Mullaghmore is being developed as a National Park.

The valleys between the hills in the Burren have a wealth of wild flowers in the limited areas of earth cover, including spring gentian and various orchids, which attract many different species of butterfly. The pearl-bordered fritillary is widely distributed in the Burren – it was at Cloncoose that the insect was first discovered in Ireland, in 1922.

The marsh fritillary favours the low-lying parts of the area, while the brown hairstreak is found around the low blackthorn scrub to the north-east. The brown hairstreak has small tails on its hind-wings. These have evolved as an imitation of the butterfly's antennae and are intended to fool predators into taking hold of the wrong end of the insect. Even if they are damaged, some butterflies can survive with half their wings missing.

Other scarce Irish species at this site include the brimstone, dingy skipper and small blue. The wood white, dark green fritillary and grayling have also been sighted here. Among the commoner species, the large, small and green-veined whites, orange tip, small tortoiseshell, peacock, speckled wood, wall, meadow brown, ringlet, small heath, small copper and common blue have all been seen in the area. Look out for females of the common blue which show the stronger blue colouring typical of western populations of this butterfly species.

61   KILLARNEY NATIONAL PARK

LOCATION *Co Kerry*; **large areas of lake shore, oakwood and mountains south of the town, off the N71.**

Ross Island, the Muckross estate and much of Lough Leane consist of a mixture of broad-leaved woodland, scrub and pasture. The long, winding ascent of the N71 has rhododendron and holly at the lower levels but climbs mainly through oak forest, finally reaching open moorland at Lough Looscaunagh, just 2 miles short of the summit at Moll's Gap.

The holly blue, wood white, silver-washed fritillary and green hairstreak can be seen relatively easily on Ross Island or the Muckross Abbey estate, and you may glimpse the occasional gatekeeper. Look for marsh fritillaries in the pastures.

At Torc, silver-washed fritillaries, holly blues and elusive purple hairstreaks inhabit the woods, while the more open parts support green hairstreaks. The male of this species has tiny areas of scent scales on the fore-wing. These patches break up as the male courts the female, releasing a fine dust that contains pheromones – complex chemicals which can induce a behavioural change in members of the same species. In this instance, the dust is thought to have an aphrodisiac effect on the females. In some species – for example, the silver-washed fritillary – the scent scales appear as dark areas on the butterfly's fore-wing. Female butterflies, too, exude pheromones to attract males. You can sometimes see green hairstreaks around Lough Looscaunagh – which is a good site, too, for large heath and marsh fritillary. In areas closer to Killarney look for whites, browns, small tortoiseshell, peacock, red admiral and small copper.

62   SHERKIN AND CAPE CLEAR

LOCATION *Co Cork*; **large inhabited islands off the south-west coast of Co Cork, accessible by boat from Baltimore; 25 minutes to Sherkin, 50 minutes to Clear Island. There is an Outdoor Pursuit Centre on Sherkin.**

Sherkin is very much a continuation of the rough ground with which west Cork abounds, having damp valley floors, steep-sided hills with some broad-leaved scrub, and exposed moorland heights. Cape Clear is more exposed – it is the southernmost point of Irish soil apart from the Fastnet Rock, 4 miles to the south-west – and consists mainly of hill pasture and moorland. There are some sheltered areas in the narrow neck between the north and south harbours, and boggy land to the west.

Because of its terrain, Sherkin has much the same range of butterfly species you would expect to find on the mainland: healthy populations of holly blue in spring and late summer, green hairstreak, marsh fritillary, dark green fritillary and gatekeeper. The silver-washed fritillary is only a chance visitor here, but you may see plenty of the more common whites and browns (with the exceptions of wood whites, large heaths and ringlets), small coppers, common blues, small tortoiseshells and peacocks. The outlying position of Sherkin makes it a prime location for migrants like the red admiral, the painted lady and, in most years, the clouded yellow.

Cape Clear, too, is favoured by these migrants – there have been years when it was the only place in Ireland to record clouded yellows. Two rare butterflies which have also been recorded here are the pale clouded yellow and the monarch.

63 BLACKWATER AND BRIDE ESTUARY

LOCATION *Co Waterford*; **woodland and coastal land on both sides of the estuary, stretching from Youghal on the N25 to Lismore on the N72.**

The hills in this area have much deciduous woodland and the oak-woods around Lismore and south-east of Tallow are the best places to see three typical woodland species – the rare purple hairstreak, holly blue and silver-washed fritillary. You may see the occasional brimstone on the margins of the woodland, but look higher up the hills among the gorse and brambles for green hairstreaks and down in the damp meadows for the scarcer marsh fritillary.

Gatekeepers, graylings and dark green fritillaries like the rough ground near the coast, as do small blues, which have been recorded at Kinsalebeg. The road from Kinsalebeg to Youghal lies close to the sea, but is well sheltered and therefore attracts a good variety of common butterflies along with migrant red admirals, painted ladies and clouded yellows. A much rarer migrant, the pale clouded yellow, has been recorded further inland near the Bride-Blackwater confluence.

Weather has a significant effect on butterfly populations and neither the clouded yellow nor the pale clouded yellow – migrants from the warmer countries of Europe – are able to tolerate the damp winter weather in Ireland, although the pale clouded yellow has been known to survive at quite low temperatures.

Both of these species feed on the nectar of lucerne, which is also known as alfalfa. This plant is widely cultivated for fodder throughout Europe and therefore ensures a plentiful supply of food for these insects.

64 BALLYTEIGE BURROWS

LOCATION *Co Wexford*; **sandhills on the south Wexford coast extending to the north-west of Kilmore Quay around Ballyteige Bay.**

This impressive range of high sandhills sweeps away from the village of Kilmore Quay for 8 miles. Sheltered hollows sustain carpets of wild flowers, whilst bramble-covered hedgerows and areas of knapweed further enhance the habitat for insect life.

In high summer, large and impressive dark green fritillaries are numerous. Most fritillaries are butterflies which inhabit woodland environments. Their speckled colouring camouflages them as they flutter across the areas of light and dark created by the sun filtering down through the trees. The dark green fritillary, however, does not live exclusively in woodland and can be found in open meadows. The caterpillars of this species have spines on their bodies – possibly a defence against parasitic wasps. Combined with body movements, the spines enable the caterpillar to deter an egg-laying wasp.

You will often find swarms of the smaller butterflies here, including common blues and small heaths. Where there is kidney vetch growing on the dunes, it is well worth seeking out the small blue. Later in the summer there should be abundant graylings and, on the verges of nearby lanes, gatekeepers. Here, as on most of the south Wexford coast, sheltered areas of flowers will hold mixed populations of small tortoiseshells, peacocks and various whites, together with migratory red admirals, painted ladies and, in favourable years, clouded yellows. A few Camberwell beauties, rare in Ireland, have also been seen.

The life cycle of the butterfly

Butterflies begin life as an egg. After a period of time that can range from days to months, the egg hatches into a caterpillar which spend most of its time eating. When the caterpillar has absorbed the necessary amount of nutrients, it changes into the chrysalis. Inside the chrysalis, the cells rearrange themselves into the adult insect. The whole process is known as a complete metamorphosis. The adult insect spends its short life mating and laying eggs to produce the next generation.

Eggs

The eggs of butterflies may be brightly coloured or covered in hairs. Some have keels (ridges) running down the sides. Patterns, designs and numbers of keels are a useful aid to identification but you will also need a strong magnifying glass. Eggs may be laid in groups – like those of the small tortoiseshell butterfly, which lays them in a pile – or singly   like those of the white admiral, which are laid on the edge of a suitable leaf. Butterflies usually spend a lot of time finding the right food plant to lay their eggs on, so that the caterpillars will have a supply of food when they hatch. However, before they can reach hatching stage, as many as 99 per cent of eggs may be killed by birds, other insects, or by disease.

Caterpillars: the eating stage

Caterpillars of butterflies are far more numerous than the adult insects that they eventually become. The great majority are eaten by birds or other predators, or die of natural infections caused by bacteria, viruses and fungi. They live concealed among vegetation, in bark crevices or in the soil and often feed at night to avoid danger. Many caterpillars disguise themselves on leaves, using both shape and colour as forms of camouflage, while others notify predators that they are poisonous with bright colours.

The caterpillar is the main eating stage of the butterfly, as the adult insect survives on a little plant nectar, or even on no food at all. In spring and summer thousands of species of caterpillar, varying greatly in colour and shape, may be found in hedgerows and trees, eating leaves, fruits and stems. Even in winter some caterpillars lurk deep in grass tussocks, feeding during the cold weather. Others go into hibernation and resume eating in spring. During this eating stage caterpillars increase in size and must shed their old tough skins four times. Each new skin is soft and allows the caterpillar to grow before it dries as a hard external skeleton.

Caterpillar jaws move sideways and are solidly built to cope with the tough leaves – or even bark – that they eat. The correct food plant of each species is recognised by chemical receptors in the cells of the hairs around the caterpillar's face rather than by sight. They have only simple eyes at the side of the face, which cannot see detail but can detect light and dark and which help the caterpillar to find its way around a plant – light means up and dark means down. Along the sides of the body are elliptical entrances called spiracles – often brightly coloured – through which the caterpillar breathes. Butterfly caterpillars move around by means of three sets of legs: the six front, or 'true' legs, will become the six legs of the adult. There are also eight prolegs set further back and a pair of claspers at the 'tail', equipped with tiny hooks that enable the caterpillar to grapple onto twigs and leaves.

The chrysalis: transformation stage

The chrysalis is the stage during which an insect is transformed from a caterpillar into an adult of a totally different shape.

Chrysalises are formed only by insects which have a complete, four-stage metamorphosis – that is, egg, caterpillar, chrysalis and adult. They are often difficult to identify because many species look the same. Those in the soil, for example, are usually a uniform brown. In their chrysalis stage butterflies go through a change in form. 'Organiser cells' move about the soup-like contents, forming the vital parts of the adult's body. Just before hatching the colours of the wings may be visible. Some butterfly species produce silk at this stage, which is used for support – the chrysalis is held close to a plant stem by a silk girdle and pad. Some species, like the white admiral, have no girdle, but hang simply from a pad. The silk can also provide extra protection by being woven into a tough cocoon. Other forms of protection during the chrysalis stage of development include reflective surfaces or marks which confuse birds by scattering light, as in the red admiral, or the growth of spines and tubercules on the casing which help in camouflage and give protection from birds and lizards. Emerging from a chrysalis is a critical time for an adult insect. The small tortoiseshell, which can take up to two hours drying its wings after emerging is particularly vulnerable to predators.

Adult butterflies

Butterflies have three pairs of legs and two pairs of wings. In most butterflies the wings will be many times their body size and covered in tiny scales, in rows, that give butterflies their colour. Each scale is pegged into a socket, but as the butterfly ages, the scales dislodge and are shed in a fine dust, often giving the butterfly a shabby, ragged appearance. In the blue butterflies, the beautiful iridescent colours are caused by the sun diffracting

Getting to know butterflies

off minute corrugations on the surface of the scales, absorbing all colours of the spectrum except blue. The white colouring in the wings of butterflies is caused by excretory pigments, similar to the white in bird droppings, which are pumped into the wings. (As butterflies eat very little, they do not excrete in the usual way).

Butterflies are equipped with a pair of antennae to analyse smells and feel the surface on which the insect stands. Their tongue or proboscis is for drinking the nectar of the flowers and stays curled up like a watch spring when not in use. Antennae are the butterfly equivalents of noses and usually have knobs at the end, distinguishing them from the feathery antennae displayed by many moths. The antennae of the large skipper, however, differ in being slightly hooked at the tip. Like all insects, butterflies have compound eyes made from thousands of photoreceptors which respond to movement in the vicinity. Butterflies are comparatively slow-flying insects – they beat their wings probably less than ten times a second – and therefore need far fewer photoreceptors in their eyes than fast-flying insects like dragonflies.

Sitting quietly on a downland slope or a grassy moor on a summer's day is a delightful introduction to the subject of butterflies. As butterflies in their myriad colours flutter over the grass, you will begin to see the close association between these insects and the plants on which they depend for food and shelter.

Every small area of Britain has a different population of insects, depending on its soil, its rainfall, the plants that grow there and the amount of sunshine it receives. And a fascinating hobby can grow out of identifying as many butterflies as possible, together with the plants they feed and breed on.

There are so many different types of butterflies in the countryside that it is impossible to remember all those that you might see on a day's outing. So keep this notebook with you to record the date, place, habitat and species seen on each outing. It can be added to each time you go out, and will serve as a reference.

Maps of insect distribution which appear in natural history books such as this all start at a local level. They are built up from information submitted by field naturalists – both amateurs and professionals – to the Natural Environment Research Council at the Institute of Terrestrial Ecology at Monks Wood Experimental Station, Abbots Ripton, Huntingdon, Cambs PE17 2LS.

The Institute enters the records in its computer and regularly issues up-dated maps. Comparing current and old maps can reveal whether a species is contracting or expanding its range. The Council issues record cards giving a check list of insects such as butterflies, moths, bumble-bees and beetles which are likely to be seen throughout Britain. Anyone who is seriously interested in recording insects may apply to the Institute. The cards are

filled in and returned at the end of the year for the records to be up-dated.

A butterfly monitoring scheme is also organised from the Institute by the Biological Records Centre. A selection of amateur naturalists send in weekly counts of butterflies seen along a regularly walked path in their localities each year. The reports help to keep an accurate assessment of what is happening to butterfly population nationally. It provides information about the spread of migrants, such as the red admiral and painted lady, across the country each year, and it records the fluctuation in the numbers of native species in a locality.

Techniques and equipment

One of the most important pieces of equipment to carry in the field is a hand lens. Lenses are available in different magnifications and can be bought from good photography shops. A lens which magnifies the image seven times is suitable for most purposes, and can be tied on a ribbon around the neck for easy access.

It is used by placing it against the eye – rather than against the insect – then bringing eye and insect together. Hand lenses are used for studying small creatures such as caterpillars and butterfly eggs.

Most larger insects, such as butterflies, can be identified in the field, and there is no need to catch them.

A butterfly net is for flying insects. To avoid injuring a butterfly after catching it, you should flip the bag of the net over the hard edge. The butterfly can then be studied through the net, or taken out carefully and examined. A sweep net, which has a straight, heavy side for dragging through long grass is used for collecting caterpillars. A beating tray is held under hedgerows and overhanging branches while you give the plant a single hard blow with a stick. It catches caterpillars and other insects as they fall.

All this equipment can be obtained from Watkins and Doncaster, Conghurst Lane, Four Throws, Hawkhurst, Kent TN18 5EZ, or Worldwide Butterflies Ltd, Compton House, near Sherborne, Dorset DT9 4QN.

Photographing insects

Most butterflies do not wait to be photographed. The picture must be taken as soon as possible before they move out of range. Knowledge of the insect's behaviour will help you to decide how close you can approach without disturbing it. Stealth and patience are also needed. You may, for example, have to focus on a flower, and then sit and wait for the moment when you can capture the momentary visit of a butterfly.

Fixed-lens or non-reflex cameras can be used to take pictures of butterflies and some models have a close-up lens that can be fitted. If you become seriously interested in photographing insects, however, you will need a single-lens reflex camera. With this type of camera, the scene that you see through the viewfinder is exactly what you photograph. It can be fitted with different sizes of lens for different types of work. Bayonet fittings are best for quick action.

For close-ups the best lens is a 'macro' of 90–100 mm or., alternatively an 80–200 mm zoom. To obtain greater magnification for smaller butterflies, such as blues and skippers, these lenses can be used with a set of three automatic extension tubes, fitted between the lens and the camera body. A 135 mm telephoto lens can also be used with extension tubes, allowing the photographer to take the picture from a greater distance, not to alarm the insect.

To obtain a 'sharp' picture, insects should ideally be photographed in direct sunlight, but many live in the shade of woodland or undergrowth, and need to be photographed with electronic flash. Two small flash guns mounted on either side of the camera, or a more expensive ring flash, will give even dispersal of light.

To photograph caterpillars or butterfly eggs, you will need a bellows. This is an extendable box which is fitted like extension tubes, but must be mounted on a tripod. It gives extremely large magnification but is probably best used indoors with electronic flash.

Safeguarding insects

Codes of practice have been drawn up to safeguard insects in various habitats. For example, you are not permitted to collect or kill insects in nature reserves. *Visiting National Nature Reserves* can be obtained from the Nature Conservancy Council, Northminster House, Peterborough PE1 1UA.

The Code for Insect Collecting, published by the Joint Commission for the Conservation of British Insects, governs the numbers of insects that can be taken, the use of light traps, and ways in which the environment should be respected. It can be obtained from the Royal Entomological Society of London, 41 Queen's Gate, London SW7 5HU.

Breeding butterflies

Butterflies can be bred at home all year round, and far greater success can be achieved than if they were breeding in the wild where eggs, caterpillars and chrysalises are eaten by predators.

The simplest way is to buy mail-order chrysalises from Worldwide Butterflies, Compton House, near Sherborne, Dorset DT9 4QN; or Entomological Livestock Supplies, Unit 3, Beaver Park, Hayeseech Road, Halesowen, West Midlands; or the Living World, Exceat Barn, Exceat, Seaford, East Sussex BN25 4AD.

The same companies also supply eggs which you can rear through the caterpillar and chrysalis stages. But first ensure a supply of food plants, perhaps in the garden or in nearby woods. It may be necessary to grow potted plants from seed.

Small tortoiseshell and peacock butterflies are quite easy to breed, and the caterpillars eat stinging nettles which can be dug up and replanted in pots. Small copper caterpillars can be reared on potted sorrels, and common blues on bird's-foot-trefoil.

Remember that you may have to look after caterpillars for six weeks, and that this period should not clash with holidays.

Where to start

Breeding can begin with any of the four stages of the butterfly's life. You may come across a mass of eggs or some caterpillars in the garden or dig up some chrysalises when turning the soil. But you must be prepared for disappointing results. You may spend weeks, for example, caring for caterpillars which eventually grow into sawflies.

Alternatively, a pair of adult butterflies may be captured and temporarily put into a cage to breed. A plant that the caterpillars will eat when they hatch should be placed in the cage to encourage the female to lay her eggs on the leaves. A captured female will often have mated already, in which case there is no need for the male.

Make the cage by putting the plant into a 12 or 15 in. flower pot filled with potting compost. Make a framework of two or three wire hoops pushed down inside the pot, and cover it with muslin.

The butterflies themselves must also be given food. Dip pink or blue cotton wool into a solution of honey and water (a teaspoon of honey in half a cup of water) and place it in a small dish on the compost.

Put the cage in direct sunshine. Once the eggs have been laid, the butterflies can be liberated into the garden. The eggs will develop on the food plant.

Caring for the caterpillars

When the caterpillars hatch from their eggs, transfer them to a clean plastic sandwich box. Lift them with a soft paint brush and put them in the box with a supply of tender young leaves from their food plant. Put the lid back on the box to prevent their escape and place it out of direct sunlight. There will be sufficient air in the box for them to breathe between daily feeds. Do not allow condensation to built up on the inside of the box as tiny caterpillars drown easily.

Change the leaves every day and also remove the droppings when they build up.

As the caterpillars grow bigger – after about a week – move them into a larger breeding cage or divide them into several boxes. Breeding cages can be brought from Watkins and Doncaster, Conghurst Lane, Four Throws, Hawkhurst, Kent or Worldwide Butterflies. Alternatively, a cage can be made by covering a wooden frame, about 2 ft × 2 ft × 2 ft, with muslin.

When the chrysalis is formed

Many chrysalises have to be kept over winter, their normal hibernation period. Keep them on damp potting compost, blotting paper or moss. Check the cage every week or so, and when the compost begins to dry out spray it with water. Keep the cage out-doors in the shade, perhaps in a shed.

When it emerges, the butterfly will need something to crawl up and expand its wings while they dry. So put some twigs inside the cage, standing up against the side. If no support is provided, the butterfly's wings are likely to dry in a crippled state.

Freeing the butterflies

Release butterflies during sunny weather, preferably near flowers to provide nectar and food plants on which the females will lay eggs. Choose a time when there are no birds near by.

Releasing butterflies is helpful to butterfly conservation, but should not be done without notifying the local conservation trust. They need to know if insects are released in a different region from where they were obtained, so that their studies of insect distribution are not confused.

Rearing caterpillars on a plant

Raising caterpillars actually on their food plant saves the daily work of changing the food supply. Create a 'sleeve' on a low branch by wrapping muslin around it. Put the caterpillars inside the sleeve and tie it at both ends. Move the caterpillars to a new branch when they have stripped the leaves.

Some caterpillars will form a chrysalis in summer. Others will spend winter as caterpillars and form chrysalises in the spring.

Skin rashes

Remember that some caterpillars can cause skin rashes, as some people are allergic to their hairs.

It is probably safest to avoid touching any hairy caterpillars with your bare hands, or if you do touch them to wash your hands immediately afterwards.

How to make your garden attract butterflies

Going out into the countryside to observe butterflies in the wild is a fascinating pastime, and it is easy to forget that you may be able to see many of the species listed in this book closer to home. A typical suburban garden can attract more than 20 species of butterfly over a few seasons, with the added bonus that a garden full of flowers becomes a haven for honey-bees and bumble-bees.

Flowers with a rich store of nectar are a magnet to butterflies. As a butterfly's natural food source is found in the wild, it helps to interplant British wild flowers among more traditional garden plants. Packets of wild flower seeds are widely available from seed-merchants and garden centres.

Butterflies will be attracted to quite different parts of the garden. Mixed borders, rough areas of lawn, rock gardens, kitchen gardens, hedges, wild gardens and orchards all offer rich habitats.

Mixed borders

Banked-up flowers in a mixed border facing the sun will attract butterflies. A brick wall behind the border will heat up in the sun, and many butterflies, including peacocks, speckled woods and walls will settle there to bask in the warmth.

Roses are not particularly attractive to butterflies, but they can be interplanted with clematis, loganberries, raspberries and cultivated blackberries, which are. Aristocrat butterflies will feed on asters, daisies and chrysanthemums in summer, and skippers are attracted to red zinnias.

The buddleia is known as the butterfly bush because of its power to attract butterflies. In July and August the long flower-spikes provide nectar for white butterflies, aristocrats, some of the browns and occasionally a fritillary.

Ice plants, which flower late into the autumn, attract small tortoiseshells and painted ladies. There are several species, but *Sedum spectabile* is the best.

Michaelmas daisies also attract butterflies in late summer and autumn, but the old-fashioned, single-flowered varieties are more effective than the double-flowered forms.

Rough areas of lawn

If your garden is big enough, leave a part of the lawn to be cut only twice each year – in early summer and autumn – and wild flowers will spring up. They can even be introduced into a lawn by sowing packeted seed in an area that has been scarified with a rake. A flush of daisies will attract small heath butterflies, and the big flowers of dandelions are likely to bring peacocks and whites. Boggy areas may support cuckoo flowers, whose pale pink flowers attract the orange tip. Later in the summer, any ox-eye daisies will tower over the grasses, taking the place of the small daisies. Blue vetch struggling up through the grass may lure passing butterflies.

Rock gardens

Many small plants, suitable for rock gardens, are attractive to butterflies. The annual cycle starts with primula and crocuses to bring the spring butterflies such as brimstones.

Later in the spring come the mauve masses of aubrietia, the white of perennial candytuft, and the yellow of *Alyssum saxatile*. Decorative varieties of thyme flower in dense clusters of red, yellow and pink through the summer.

Towards the winter, make sure there is some ivy in your garden. It not only provides food for caterpillars of the holly blue but makes a good hibernation site for the brimstone. Brimstones will also visit the purple flowers of periwinkle.

Kitchen garden

Cabbages, cauliflowers, brussels sprouts and broccoli all bring cabbage white butterflies to lay their eggs on the leaves. However, much as you want to encourage these butterflies, you will not want their caterpillars to eat the vegetables before you can. If you plant tomatoes or wormwood nearby, the strong smell will deter the butterflies and excess leaves pruned off tomato plants and laid on the growing cabbages will also deter whites.

Vegetable gardens will attract many insects more desirable than cabbage whites. Blue butterflies will feed on the nectar of pea, bean and raspberry flowers and you can encourage butterflies to visit radishes, if you let them run to seed.

Hedges

Hedges are a constant source of flowers for butterflies. In February and March, sloe (blackthorn) flowers come out before the leaves, supplying nectar to butterflies waking from winter hibernation. In May and early June, hawthorn hedges and trees can be covered in cascades of white or pink blossom. Hedges of virburnum, privet and choisy are all good sources of nectar for butterflies during the summer.

The wild garden

If a sunny area of the garden is left to grow wild, it will become an insect haven. Clumps of nettles should be left to encourage peacocks and small tortoiseshells to lay their eggs. The purple flowers of thistles are also attractive to aristocrat butterflies, as well as whites and brimstones. Scabious and knapweeds attract blue, copper and brown butterflies to their nectar. Vetches which scramble up through the grass also attact blue butterflies and cowslips and primroses may attract the Duke of Burgundy fritillary.

Index

Acknowledgments

Butterflies is based on the Reader's Digest *Nature Lover's Library Field Guide to the Butterflies and Other Insects of Britain* to which the following made major contributions:

Principal consultant and author Dr John Feltwell, F.R.E.S., F.L.S., M.I. Biol.
Other consultants Dr Keith Porter; Anthony Wootton.

Artists Stephen Adams; David Baird; Rachel Birkett, M.A.; Dick Bonson; Leonora Box; Wendy Bramall; Josiane Campan; Jeane Colville, B.A; Kevin Dean; Colin Emberson; Pat Flavel; Brenda Katte; Norman Lacey, M.I.S.T.C.; Richard Lewington; Line Maiihé; Guy Michel; Tricia Newell; Liz Pepperell; Sandra Pond, L.S.I.A.D. -E.A.C; Elizabeth Rice, S.W.L.A.; Jim Russell; Ann Savage; Helen Senior; Sally Smith; Barbara Walker; Adrian Williams.

Cartography The distribution maps of butterflies are based on information supplied by The Biological Records Centre of The Institute of Terrestrial Ecology, and were prepared by Clyde Surveys Limited, Maidenhead.

The publishers wish to thank the following for contributions and invaluable help towards producing *Butterflies*:
Michael J. Woods (English, Scottish, Welsh and Northern Irish sites)
J. Paul Hillis (sites in the Republic of Ireland)

Keith Alexander (Zoologist on the Biological Survey Team) and Katherine Hearn (Adviser on Conservation) from the National Trust

The Royal Society for Nature Conservation

The National Trust
for Places of Historic Interest or Natural Beauty
36 Queen Anne's Gate, London SW1H 9AS

The National Trust for Scotland
5 Charlotte Square, Edinburgh EH2 4DU

An Taisce (The National Trust for Ireland)
The Tailors' Hall, Back Lane, Dublin 8.

16−032−1